TRAVELS IN THE EAST

TRAVELS
IN THE
EAST

Donald Richie

with a Foreword by Stephen Mansfield

Stone Bridge Press • Berkeley, California

Published by
Stone Bridge Press
P. O. Box 8208
Berkeley, CA 94707
sbp@stonebridge.com • www.stonebridge.com

Some of this text was originally printed in *The Japan Times*, *Winds*, *The New York Times*, *The Hudson Review*, *The Partisan Review*, *The San Francisco Examiner*, *House and Garden*, *East/West*, *Brick*, *Newsweek*, *TIME*, *Partial Views* (Japan Times Press), *The Donald Richie Reader* (Stone Bridge Press), *The Scarlet Gang of Asakusa* by Yasunari Kawabata: Introduction (University of California Press), *The Nightless City* (by J. E. de Becker): Introduction (reprint, Stone Bridge Press).

The original visits were: Egypt (2001); India (1988); Bhutan (1997); Mongolia (2004); China (1989); Laos (1999); Cambodia (2001); Vietnam (1996); Thailand: Sukothai (2005), Mae Hong Son (2006), Krabi (2001); Burma (2007); Borneo (1995); Korea (1988); Yap (2004); Japan: Ryoan-ji (1963), Koya-san (1990), Hokkaido (1990), Satsuma (1991), Noto Hanto (1993), Kunisaki (1991), Asakusa (2005).

The stanza from "Ithaka" is from *Collected Poems* by C. P. Cavafy, translated by Edmund Keeley and Philip Sherrard (Princeton University Press). The quote from Claude Lévi-Strauss is from *Tristes Tropiques*, translated by John and Doreeen Weightman (Jonathan Cape, Ltd.). The Flaubert quotes are from *Flaubert in Egypt*, translated and edited by Francis Steegmuller (Academy Chicago Publishers). The Kafka quote is from *The Complete Stories*, translated by Willa and Edwin Muir (Schocken Books). The Victor Segalen quote is from *René Leys*, translated by J. A. Underwood (Overlook Press).

Cover photograph by Michael F. Vardaro, Scripps Institution of Oceanography.

Manufactured in the United States of America

LIBRARY OF CONGRESS CATALOGING-IN-PUBLICATION
Richie, Donald, 1924–.

  Travels in the East / Donald Richie; with a foreword by
Stephen Mansfield.
    p. cm.
  ISBN 978-1-933330-61-7
  1. Asia—Description and travel. I. Title.
  DS10.R53 2007
  915'.04429—dc22

                              2007040608

FOR DAE-YUNG

Ithaka gave you the marvelous journey.
Without her you wouldn't have set out.
She has nothing left to give you now.

C. P. Cavafy

Contents

Foreword

In a different age, one of audacious maritime or overland exploration, let's say, Donald Richie would not have sailed the Spanish Main, nor sought entry to Mecca in the robes of a Muslim Hajji. Unlike the Roman traveler and diarist Egeria, he would not have tried to travel the whole of the known world, followed the bloodstained traders of the Congo into hearts of darkness, or seduced blackamoors in the impecunious beach hovels of Zanzibar. He would not have lusted after El Dorado.

The *gout du gouffre*, "the taste for the abyss" — Baudelaire's phrase, Rimbaud's affliction and undoing — may not be an absolute prerequisite for today's travel writer, yet there remains a peculiar, very contemporary prejudice against people who travel in comfort, a misconception that nothing worthwhile can come from those, like Richie, for whom travel is a supreme, unabashed pleasure. The novelist Martin Amis, questioning the integrity of the late Bruce Chatwin, arguably the foremost travel writer of his generation, felt vindicated after catching sight of a sleeping-bag the author had left behind somewhere, "a very dinky little sleeping bag with a Club Class sticker." That, he concluded, "just about sums him up." It didn't, of course, and Amis soon enough revised his opinion once he met, and more important, read the man.

For today's travel writer, life is complicated by the

demands of editors and literary agents, who expect travel accounts to be triumphs of the human spirit, to feature record-breaking feats, promotional gimmicks or stunts, to include at the very least the use of some eccentric mode of transport, before their work can even be considered for publication. Titles like *On Sledge and Horseback to Outcast Siberian Lepers* and *To Lake Tanganyika in a Bath Chair*, both written by redoubtable Victorian travelers, are early examples of the genre. More recent books have been written on subjects ranging from hang-gliding in Bangladesh, to walking Burma's insurgent trails, to navigating the length of the Mekong by inner tube. In Richie's travel essays, gathered at long last in book form, we rely less on the Sisyphean ordeals some writers lay claim to than on an even more extraordinary phenomenon: good writing.

Famously refractory to definition, travel writing has been called cultural voyeurism, the practiced art of dissimulation, a sub-species of memoir, simulated estrangement, the ultimate document of the self in transit. Most authors in this field explore a world that is essentially external. The best travel writers, I would hazard, are introspectives, people who, as they cover the ground outwardly, advance inwardly. Richie is such a writer, his authority as a chronicler grounded in a memory and interest in what others have chosen to forget, or ignore, in their pursuit of travel as a quick fix or thrill.

Richie gives us that unaccountable jolt of elation, a surcharge of glucose to the imagination that only truly transcendental travel writing can engender. And, like the best accounts, these essays inspire restlessness, a desire to verify and sample. Almost everyone with the requisite means travels these days, of course, and Asia is one of the great destinations. Who among us can resist the opportunity, after all, to exchange a walk to the subway for air miles, metaphysical jungles for real ones, to trade in musty Arcadia for the new Nirvanas?

Not that Richie claims to have discovered any untrodden destinations in this anthology. Many of the places the author writes about were ruined or debauched long before the first of these accounts were written. The ancient shadow play, no rival to the sensuality of film, had all but passed into memory by then; native dress, for centuries the preserve of Asian peasantry and royalty, acquired new uses when worn by flight attendants. A gift of freshly picked Champa flowers were no longer sufficient to gain admittance to a Laotian performance of the Hindu dance epics. As for notions of virtuous poverty, they were already as rare as sightings of the Himalayan snow leopard.

If the modern anxiety concerns vanishing cultures, vanishing cities, vanishing tribes, Richie's concern is about vanishing essence. The retrieval of essence, the spirit of place, is accomplished through reproducing the textuality of the travel experience, something that only literature can convey. Richie's carefully composed and textured work—aerated, full of sunshine and graduated shadow—resembles, to appropriate a phrase from André Malraux, a "museum without walls," that is, an open exposition of land forms, native people, aesthetic artifacts, newly encountered cultures that, regardless of tireless intrusion, can seem like newly minted worlds. The subjects of these essays are not merely reimagined destinations, but departure points for reflection on the meaning of travel. The novelist John Gardner once remarked that in literature there are only two plots. You go on a journey, or a stranger comes to town. Travelers who also happen to be writers, literary sightseers, are fortunate: They can find parts to their liking in both plots.

Few travelers find in their homecomings the promise of a deeper journey. It is fitting that this book, after roaming the far corners of Asia, should conclude with a matchless ensemble of pieces on Japan, the author's home. It was Horace who, using verse to chide a friend for his feckless, compulsive travels, wrote, "You go in ships in search of bliss, yet what you seek is here in Ulubrae, you'll find, if to your search you bring a balanced mind."

It may very well be that in Japan Richie has discovered the very best landfall of all—his Ulubrae.

Stephen Mansfield
Japan, 2007

Introduction

To travel . . . what does that mean? The dictionary gives
one definition: to go on from place to place or visit various
places and countries for business or pleasure. But there are as
well many other things to be said about travel.

Edward Said observed that "the more one is able to leave
one's cultural home, the more easily is one able to judge it,
and the whole world as well, with the spiritual detachment
and generosity necessary for true vision. The more easily,
too, does one assess oneself and alien cultures with the same
combination of intimacy and distance."

True vision . . . but what is that? Some have thought that
travel indicates one's real position, one determined by self.
Gustave Flaubert entertained a theory that a more proper
way of ascribing nationality would be according to the places
to which one is attracted. Rainer Maria Rilke maintained
that "we are born, so to speak, provisionally, it doesn't matter
where; it is only gradually that we compose, within ourselves,
our true place of origin, so that we may be born there retro-
spectively." And, more recently, Alain de Botton has suggested more personal reasons for travel: "If it is true that love is
a pursuit in others of qualities we lack in ourselves, then in
our love of someone from another country, one ambition may
be to weld ourselves more closely to values missing from our
own culture."

At the same time, though travel may well be a reaching out for, it is also a pushing away from. Indeed, our need to get to is often, maybe always, attached to a like imperative to get away. Certainly what we like in the new place is that it is opposite the old — Baudelaire's "anywhere, anywhere," so long as it is far from what we are leaving. The motion itself begins the process. You don't even have to get there . . . wher-ever. Already you are experiencing the invigorating *poésie des départs*.

Following after what we feel we lack leads, by defini-tion, into difference — often so different as to be perceived as *exotic*. This term the dictionary finds "strikingly unusual . . . suggesting distant countries and unfamiliar cultures," adding that this is often found "very colorful and exciting."

True, but it does not go on to include the further his-tory of the word, now downgraded into something less re-spectable — one of the reasons that it is now bad form to insist upon racial, national, personal differences. Rather, we are to suggest that every place and everyone is much the same, that we are not to be taken in by superficial discrepancy. The po-litically correct insists upon a plain surface.

When Edward Said exposed the predatory face of Ori-entalism, however, he failed to exhibit the other faces, all of them less voracious. And when the exotic is consequently castigated for being itself, then a genuine appreciation for the more profound aspects of the foreign, the alien, the other are likewise forbidden.

Yet, a liking for, a need for the exotic is one of the con-ditions under which we live. A preference for difference is a requisite for moving in any direction at all. We need not equate "the Orient" with "happiness" as Flaubert did in his early travels, but we ought to recognize that equating happiness with somewhere else is one of the prerequisites for personal progress. Along with this come the lessons that travel teaches. The exotic is by definition the unknown. We must learn about it. In this sense, all travel is a search for knowledge and all travel writing is *bildungroman*. You are what you learn and this learning extends in two direction—both where you are and who you are.

New countries are something like new clothes. I try them on—do they fit, how do they look? To be in a new place is to find a new self. Maybe that is why we love travel—we leave behind a person grown stale with familiarity, ourselves. We find, for a time at any rate, an attractive stranger, ourselves. We walk along new streets, all eyes, all ears, noticing as we never do back home, back where everything is memorized. We now see more, hear better, our attention is continually claimed and that slide into habit is postponed. We can fall into it again—the second trip down a strange street will do it—but for the moment we are free of our old self, inhabiting our new.

Even the pleasure of being lost. If experienced back home it would be horrid—insanity has finally struck. Abroad, however, it is to be expected, even courted. I wander on and on, from one exotic bypass to another, and slowly realize that, enchanted by new sights at each corner, I do not know my way back. Do I care? Not if I am an inveterate traveler. This is what I traveled for, this is but a smaller, more coherent map of my life.

For one thing, we are spared the terrors of belonging.

We do not belong while traveling. This is something that the sight of any strange street or the stare of any native will assure us. We are not members.

This can cause panic in those who feel that without membership they are no one. For others, however, this proof of independence offers liberty, the freedom to think or to act without being constrained by necessity or force. For these fortunate few, travel is freedom from captivity.

Foreigners—tourists, expatriates alike—are in an anomalous position, one strange and difficult to identify or classify. They are in the country but not of it. They are not subject to the laws of class, are immune to local strictures. Foreignness forgives almost anything they do. *They are not like us; they did not know any better.* That they are so visibly apart disarms the natives. The locals are more reassured than not and the foreigner finds himself exempt from almost everything. They can't speak properly, and even if they do their accent renders them apart.

This said, however, speaking the language considerably widens the visitor's horizon. In English, when I am happy, I am voluble—laughter, gesticulations. When I am happy in my other language, Japanese, however, I—at most—smile, arms down, hands behaving themselves. Who would I be, I wonder, in Urdu? But I will never know because I will never know Urdu. To speak a different language is to discover not only a different place but also a different self. And to not speak the language is to become no one at all.

Not to know the language in the place I am reduces me. Not only am I deaf to all the informative noise around me, I am also incapable of making any myself. I am like a very young child, or an animal. Staring about me, I find that my eyes must take the place of my tongue as I try to interpret what I see. What did that gesture mean? Yes, or no? Does that smile mean agreement, contempt?

And what about me? But that treasured and traveling self is now inside the small box of the former self. Inchoate, babbling, I am reduced, am no longer a person. Indeed, my personality (that quality based on who I think I am) has become invisible. Those around me in this new place cannot see or hear it. I remember visitors in Japan, those who depended most on language to express who they were, being driven to dejection by this enforced silence. Truman Capote turning even more petulantly childish. Anthony West driving himself out of the country in despair. Yet that is only one option—another is to revel in the freedom from self.

Flaubert said Maxime Du Camp, his traveling companion, thought that travel writing was "a low form of literature, and that he had higher aspirations. Travel should serve only to enliven one's style." And it is true that the solitude and insecurity of travel makes one ponder on such questions as who one is and leads to that self-definition, which is style. But here one must disagree with Du Camp. There is no higher aspiration.

The ways are various. Me, I seem to learn most from gazing backward, regarding the steadily vanishing forms of what once was and, through these, accommodating an understanding of the present. Thus, my vision of travel is informed by a strong sense of time passing, and here I am perhaps influenced by my living most of my life in Japan, a country that has made a hankering for the elegiac into a fine art.

But hankerings are spatial as well as temporal. Perhaps

consequently, a search for the last paradise, someplace totally different from where one is. Asia seems a possible location for such a place. It is the antipodes. If I were to dig a hole in the backyard in Ohio I would eventually emerge in the fabled East.

Everything is different because everything is opposite. And if we call where we come from bad, then we may expect not only the good but the paradisiacal. Even though I now know that paradises are polluted when we tourists swarm.

In my Eastern travels I must then appear to be anti-Western—a given, since it is the West that has first attained the financial clout that makes pollution possible. Thus I find estimable Yap's refusal of the worst of our Western century. This does not, however, make the Yapese virtuous. It merely indicates that these people have not yet attained the environmental power necessary to despoil in the name of development. But just you wait. Asia now holds most of the past because it still costs too much to get rid of it. Travel allows me to see these remains while they still exist.

This is the dimension of travel that most appeals to me—a reality different from mine is revealed. And it can be revealed only by my seeing it as a traveler.

An example—from the square window of my jet liner, I look down at the brown and distant land, and I see, inscripted in that distant sand beneath me, an indistinct but colossal square. This is something I could see only as a traveler, only from the air, looking back through the millennia—the shape of ancient Babylon.

Donald Richie

TRAVELS
IN THE
EAST

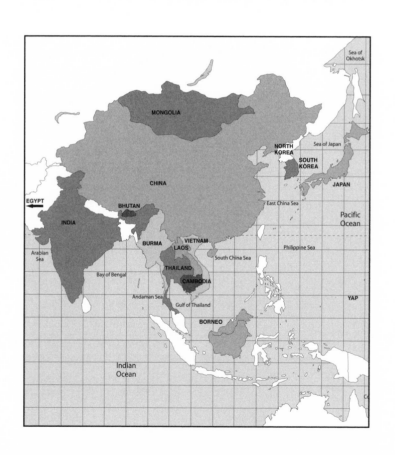

EGYPT

The Temples of the Nile

To float down the Nile, stopping at the temples, sleeping on my ship—this was my desire, and now I am in a stateroom on the Cheops I, a floating hotel, looking at the wharf at Aswan and reading Flaubert's journal of a similar voyage he made in 1849. I notice many of the same things. "The barber, dog barking, children crying, a visit *ces dames*." Well, not the latter. "The ladies" are now nowhere in evidence.

But, like him, I go to Philae, an island temple-complex devoted to Isis, and during the nineteenth century the ruins thought most romantic of all. Flaubert found it filled with "a thousand charming details" but was indignant at the religious depredations, the defacings of the ancient deities, the chisel marks of later intolerance. I find it blazing under the hot late-spring sun, Isis nursing Horus, a bas-relief so enormous that the Christian chiselers could not reach that high; below, a series of immense slanting, roofless chambers holding the sun and making the shadows cold. There are also signs of earlier tourists: the Temple of Augustus, the Gate of Diocletian, the Kiosk of Trajan.

Everything is so stunningly permanent that it is difficult to realize that this is not quite what Flaubert saw. The UNESCO only twenty-five years ago moved the entire

complex stone by stone from its original island to one somewhat like it and reconstructed Philae just as it had been. Now
it is permanently above the varying waters of the Nile, which,
thanks to dams, floods no more, and the only yearly influx
the charming Philae must now endure is the high tourist
seasons.

＊

The barber, dog, children, wharf, the entire city of Aswan suddenly slides from view. It is as though the scene is
being rolled past my proscenium — the stateroom window,
flanked by the immobile sofa, the stationary lamp, my tor-
pid suitcase. Outside, the real scenery, like the major attraction after the Aswan short subject, at once begins. It flows by
like the Nile itself: ocher hills, the desert. And against it the
viridian tracery of the *palmiers*, the eruption of a white dome,
the distant vertical of a minaret. And accompanying the tan
waves is the wash of the Muzak, caramel-colored music, so
festive, so sad.

Palms, white mud-brick huts, mosques, people plowing,
fishing — as in an ancient frieze. And I realize, like every other
tourist from Augustus on, that I am watching history unreel,
I am looking at things as they have always been. I peer back
into all those centuries that the Nile holds, I float on the long-
est river in the world (a length Flaubert did not know since it
had not yet been calculated), and I gaze at the world's most
ancient intact civilization (a fact he knew very well indeed).

I gaze. It is one thing to land in a jungle or a desert or a
strange city of which one has barely heard, but quite another

finally to land in a place about which one has heard all one's life—the books, the movies, the tube. There is already a connection. Blank strangeness is not to be expected—you have already colonized the place. Such are the expectations to be feared somewhere you think you know, like Egypt. And how soon, and how joyfully, are such complacent expectations dashed. I have merely seen these sights. Now I may experience them.

*

The Temple of Kom Ombo, in ancient times on the great caravan route from Nubia, a place where gold from the mines on the Red Sea ended up and where elephants from the interior jungles were taken to be used as defense by the army. This I had read about, but I had not seen the great river the same color as the vast sands, had not felt the texture of the cut stone, brittle but permanent, not sensed the enormous weight of the noontime sun.

The ruins are doubled, and perfectly symmetrical because of the dual nature of the place (twin courts, twin colonnades, twin sanctuaries); the temple is dedicated to falcon-headed Horus on the left and to the crocodile-headed Sobek on the right. A place consequently sacred to the saurians, with which the Nile then swarmed—four of them, mummified, are on display at the temple.

I wander in what is left of these colossal twin edifices and look warily about for crocodiles. But they are all gone, driven from the Nile by big boats such as the one on which I am now floating.

❖

Edfu—Flaubert only says that the temple "serves as public latrine for the entire village." He is much more taken with the town of Esna, just downstream. It was here that he encountered the dancer Kuchuk Hanem, "a tall, splendid creature . . . when she bends, her flesh ripples into bronze ridges." She was persuaded to dance. After the musicians had been blindfolded, she performed something called "The Bee," apparently a kind of ur-striptease involving the premise of the insect's being trapped under her burnoose. Afterward, imaginary bee expelled, now naked but for a few trinkets, "she sank down breathless on the divan, her body continuing to move slightly in rhythm."

Nothing of the sort occurs to me at Edfu, but I do get to experience the superb Temple of Horus, a huge complex that remains the largest and most completely preserved pharaonic temple in Egypt. Having taken nearly two centuries to finish (and finally completed by Cleopatra's father), it is entered through an enormous (120 feet high, says the guidebook) py-lon decorated with colossal reliefs of Ptolemy XIII pulling the hair of his enemies while Horus looks approvingly on.

When royalty and the gods are this big they tend not only to impress but also to frighten. Perhaps this is because our times equate size with terror (King Kong), but also because a feeling of awe is not untinged with a sense of danger. As I proceed further and further into the bowels of Horus, as succeeding waves of creeping colossal colonnades more and more shut out the inquiring sun, I feel ancient misgivings. And as I trail into the darkness of the sanctuary where in distant times a live falcon—Horus himself—perched and brooded, I know what this feeling is: apprehension.

❊

Safely back on board I am served tea (Prince of Wales, pear jam on fresh croissants) and then, my hotel safely anchored, take a sailboat, a *felucca*, out over the waters of the Nile, now as blue as those of the ocean, to a small nearby island, festooned with the luxuriant foliage that river water brings to desert shores.

Sails stretched, we glide under the lee beneath a sudden fall of what seems like snow but is really spores of the trees in which dozens of white egrets are nesting, treading the branches. We are also joined by a little boy in a boat not much larger than he is. He grasps the gunwales of mine and is carried along as, flat on his back, he entertains me in various languages. He can do "Home on the Range," it turns out, and perhaps mistaking my nationality but respecting his setting, "Die Lorelei." When he begins the theme song from *Titanic*, however, I pay him off and cast him away.

Then I turn to look at the verdant island, deepest green against the parched tan of the Sahara directly behind, abruptly abutting it. What is this sense of well-being that I strangely and suddenly experience? It is as though this contrast has somehow defined poles I had thought opposite, as though I am rendered whole. It is like the sun unexpectedly appearing on an otherwise cloudy day, and I am unreasonably happy.

Later I find a parallel in Flaubert. He is also on his way to Luxor. "The mountains are dark indigo, blue over dark gray

. . . the palms are black as ink, the sky is red, the Nile has the look of a lake of molten steel. . . . It was then as I was enjoying these things that I felt a surge of solemn happiness that reached out toward what I was seeing, and I thanked God in my heart for having made me capable of such a joy: I felt fortunate at the thought, and yet it seemed to me that I was thinking of nothing: it was a sensuous pleasure that pervaded my entire being."

I lie awake tonight, the ceiling crossed by the lights we pass, rocking on the bosom of the Nile. One hundred fifty years ago, a 28-year-old Flaubert felt what I, a 77-year-old, now also experience. I wonder if this is the sensuous gift that Egypt was proverbially known to bestow upon the traveler.

❄

Luxor, the 4,000-year-old site of ancient Thebes, and now the greatest open-air museum in the world. First off, the collossi of Memnon, what is left of them, standing there. Time, earthquake, and mankind have reduced these to enormous piles of tumbled stone. It was already one of the acknowledged tourist sites in the nineteenth century, but Flaubert seems to have missed it—at least he writes nothing about it.

Nor about the Valley of the Kings, a great white, dusty, blinding vale where next I go. This official city of the royal dead reminds me of Washington, D.C. with its enormous distances, its whiteness, its array of official monuments. I go into a few of them, decorated tombs, color still intact, and then ride (on a small donkey, reluctant but reasonable, named by its young owner Mickey Mouse) to the many-tiered Temple of Hatshepsut. This also Flaubert did not see, since it was not excavated until 1896 and is still being restored.

It is also now remembered as the site of the 1977 massacre when more than fifty foreign tourists were slaughtered by "terrorists"—second-tier, left-hand-side—masked machine-gunners emerging from the dark inner colonnades. No one has forgotten this—least of all, the Egyptian government. The entire Nile area from Aswan to Luxor is now reassuringly swarming with soldiers, policemen, security guards. Their phalanxes are ubiquitous, and each member is armed. Though this massive presence might give pause to some tourists, I find it heartening. Flaubert, on the other hand, could not have understood it. In his time, tourist terrorism did not exist.

❖

"The mass of the pylons and the colonnades looms in the darkness; the moon, just risen, seems resting on the horizon, low and round and motionless, just for us, and the better to illumine the horizon's great flat stretch. We wander amid the ruins, which seem immense; dogs are barking furiously on all sides, and we carry stones or bricks with us." This is Flaubert on his first evening at Luxor.

I went there earlier in the day, just as the sun was declining, wandered along the double row of ram-headed sphinxes that once formed an avenue all the way to Karnak, and into the massive funnel of ruined halls, the greatest of which was dedicated to Amun, one of the deities of creation and the most important god of Thebes. In the fading light I looked at his great pink granite obelisk, and then the empty dais of its twin. This missing column is not looking at the calm darkness of Luxor but at the endless traffic of the Place de la Concorde in Paris. Flaubert had the same thought. "How it must miss its Nile! What does it think as it watches all the cabs drive by, instead of the chariots it saw at its feet in the old days?"

*

Karnak, now only a short drive from Luxor itself, is more than a temple. It is a spectacular complex of pylons, obelisks, kiosks, sanctuaries. The guidebook tells me that ten major cathedrals could be contained in the space, and that the initial pylon is twice as high as that at Luxor.

Flaubert tells me that Karnak is "a palace of giants. The stone grills still existing in the windows give the scale of these formidable beings. As you walk about in this forest of tall columns you ask yourself whether men weren't served up whole on skewers, like larks." And all this enormity just to honor the dead.

Tonight, as Flaubert's moon again rises, I return to enormous Karnak—the most colossal, the most perfect, the most awesome. Particularly now—illuminated by shifting lights as I wander through its forest of papyrus-shaped pillars, faces millennia-old gazing down at me, surrounded by music. The score, however, is apparently by the twin brother of Maurice Jarre and reduces emotion by appropriating it. Nonetheless, kitschy as it all might have been, this *son et lumière* is saved by the mere fact that it brings one here, in the night, to ancient Karnak.

❁

In the morning, packing, leaving the boat, preparing for the flight to Cairo, I sat over a second espresso and thought about Karnak, how I had been surrounded there by all this mortality. And then it struck me that ancient Egypt was not death possessed, as is often thought. Rather, it was life possessed, as few other civilizations have been. Why else this enormous celebration of the terminus, unless one is so in love with the journey. These tombs, these sepulchers, these mummies—they attest to a life-fixation so extreme that it is as though death is defeated.

Later in the day I was on the Geza plateau looking at the pyramids, all three of them, ranging from largest to smallest: Cheops, Chephren, and Mycernus. Gazing at these wonders for just an afternoon. Shouldn't I, like an anchorite, chain myself to a corner of Cheops and spend my remaining years in contemplation, contributing my tiny arc to this vast curve of time?

Then it occurs to me that this small glimpse implies concentration. And I remember Claude Lévi-Strauss's maxim: "The most intense concentration is forced upon one by the brevity of the stay." Though I have seen the pyramids pictured, I have never before seen them so plain. There they stand, made only of stone and mud, yet swallowing up the horizon. The color of the soil, they pile sky-high, and the ocher is so intense it is like a sound.

You can go in, too. This I did not do, though my young camel driver told me I should. But it is so wonderful to be on the *outside* of the pyramids, seeing them loom, feeling, as did Flaubert, that they are "inordinately huge and completely sheer; like a cliff, like a thing of nature, a mountain."

"Three million stones, each one big as a Toyota," says my driver, referring to Cheops, as I pitch along its slope. He passes in front of me, leading my beast (named Ali Baba, I am told), and I am struck by his profile. Where can I have seen it before?

Then I remember — Philae and the teenaged Horus being nursed by Isis. The same long nose, the same stern gaze, the same brown limbs glimpsed among the folds. Is it just romantic me? I wonder. But no, a family resemblance is there. As I lurch along on Ali Baba's back and enter the cold shadow of Cheops it seems somehow marvelous, as though I am witnessing something extraordinary.

Feeling my gaze, he turns upon me his fine pharaonic regard: "OK? Sure you don't want to go in?" No, I tell him, it is enough just being there with him and Ali Baba in the shadow of Cheops, that I am happy as I am.

"You happy, I happy," says Horus.

Death defeated, life affirmed. This remains Egypt's gift. Flaubert's last thoughts on leaving Karnak will be mine on leaving Egypt: "Sadness at leaving *stones*? Why?"

INDIA

The Primordial

It looms huge on the map, that inverted mass that used to be colored colonial pink. Now, still just as large, it is dust-colored, its real shade. India is earth—soil, dirt, mud. It is where we came from, where we are going.

I sit in a small park in Calcutta—now post-colonial Kolkata—and regard a patch of this earth, part of a busy path. It is trod, as I watch, by hundreds of feet—over the years by many millions. These have reduced the soil to a surface as though baked. No longer loam, it is incapable of harboring a seed or a sprout. This is earth returned to its rocky origins, enameled with use.

Gazing, I try to recapture its colors. Claude Lévi-Strauss did this once, right here in Calcutta, and glimpsed "a continuous surface of pink and green tints . . . like the exquisite colors of some very old tapestry which has been worn threadbare by long use and tirelessly darned. This is India."

But from my level in the Calcutta park these shades, if there, are obliterated by the tireless passing of those who tread upon them. Dozens a minute, thousands an hour. Such concentration . . . how many millions, each foot pressing a city back to its geological strata.

❀

These strata are mined. At the temple of Kailasanath at Ellora, I stand as though in a deep trench, confronted by a huge shrine cut out of solid rock. The workers, more sculptors than masons, cut down from the ground, leaving a mass of rock in the middle. This they then carved into a temple, hollowed out its corridors and its chambers.

Just as Michelangelo said he found his statue in the mass of marble with which he was working, so these artists discovered their temple, just below where they were standing. And, like the Italian who said that he had liberated the figure that he found, so these Indians freed their subterranean temple and opened it to the skies.

The West constructs from a floor to supporting walls, to a roof. The East — or at least this part of it, at Ellora — is made just opposite. Digging down, the roof is found, then, under it, one by one, the pillars are revealed, beneath them are the rooms and the hallways, and, finally, the solid rock floor.

Working with what is found, these people — now well over a thousand years dead — sometimes built from the great boulders sitting on a beach. A few years ago I went to Mamallapuram, where the enormous stones, still sitting just where they had landed after some colossal catastrophe, had been cut and drilled and hollowed with an infinite patience and skill, and after a time a seaside temple emerged, dedicated to Shiva, and there it sits yet.

Inside all of these temples cut from the living rock, the walls, ceilings, pillars are sculpted, encrusted with animals, with bits of anecdote, with the gods made small. And though the stone is hard, the carvings seem strangely soft. This is because, over the centuries, they have been handled. Just as a million feet have packed down the earth, so a million hands have rubbed these carvings. Warm flesh has slowly worn down cold stone.

❉

The people — there are so many of them that I see little else. Omnipresent they are — are there really so many, or is it because they are all outside, where they are so incessantly visible?

To stand in Old Delhi is to be assailed. With so many in one place there is not enough for everyone — not enough space, not enough food. Hence the begging — hands held out, grasping children, the exposing of charity-inducing injuries or diseases.

And the stares. I stare at them and they stare at me. Into their gaze I read many things. It is as though they are dying, as though this is the one last look. And, to be sure, some of them are. Well, we all are, but these poor people are dying visibly. And there I stand, in my good clothes, with money in my pocket. Why don't they turn and rend me? But that is not their way.

I was at the great temple of Kali in Calcutta. There was apparently a festival going on — immense crowds. They filled the courts and dozens crouched by the drain around in back, to lick this black hole, this hallowed anus from which dribbled the holy remains of offered food and flowers.

Some distance away was another foreigner, a middle-aged woman in tweeds, stout shoes, sun-hat—British. She was judiciously choosing which small coin to give a beggar and the crowd surrounding her suddenly erupted.

Like a wave it fell upon her, engulfed her. I saw one hand held high, as though to spare the purse, and then it, too, disappeared into the roiling mass. I turned in consternation to my guide.

"Do not be alarmed," he said, adding that they would not hurt her, indeed that they meant no harm, rather that each thought that maybe she would give a small coin to them as well and that this had excited them. Nor would they steal. But then he said I should never give alms in public.

And when the crowd had ebbed, there she was, a woman who had survived a tidal wave. The sun-hat was gone but the purse was still there, clutched in her hand. The crowd drifted away, but there she still stood.

*

In Calcutta I was taken out by a lady kindly acting as hostess. She was one of the Rays, a prominent and wealthy Calcutta family, and she said she would show me the real India. To this end she told the chauffeur where to go, and soon we were riding through narrow streets and being stared at as we passed.

We were going to a poor native market she knew, because the *chapati* pancakes were actually better than those at the Imperial, where I was staying. The taste of the real India seemed a good place to start.

Parked, the limousine was at once surrounded, people

pressing against the car, patting it, pushed up to the windows. A child was told by the driver to bring the chapatis, and the window was quickly rolled back up.

We in the back seat were ignoring the crowds pressing against the windows and staring. We were talking about Proust—about the final party and the revelation of the new Princesse de Guermantes—when the child returned with the pancakes and the driver rolled down the window to pay for them.

As soon as the money was seen the limousine heaved and soon began to rock as those outside crowded nearer, perhaps thinking that alms were forthcoming. Some became excited. A small boy climbed on the hood; a man with an ulcered face pushed himself to the windshield and wiped it with his head.

They were quiet and, in their way, orderly, but the chauffeur started his motor with a roar and my hostess began to cry. Then she opened the window and held her purse out upside-down. The small coins rained and the crowd began rolling about in an effort to retrieve them. We lurched off and she turned to me, eyes damp, purse in a clenched fist, and said: *Sometimes it gets to you.*

❋

In a street stall near the Kalikut Botanical Garden I saw an astonishing baby. It was 2 or 3 years old and was lying on its back, legs open, and it was made up. Its eyes were large and lustrous with thick black kohl fringes, a seductive look. It was more monstrous than beautiful, however. Its position, flat on its back, legs open, and those eyes seemed to me to suggest untoward possibilities—further horrors. A small houri? *Was it for sale or what?* I asked my Indian companion. *Oh, no,* she said with a smile: They believe that kohl prevents ophthalmia.

❊

The visitor sees what the visitor expects to see. There are those who come to India to experience the Raj, and so that is what they do. They come to New Delhi and expect Victorian colonial architecture, and this is what they see. This is also apparently all that they see. Unless you are protected by some such use for India, however, you are at its mercy.

I had come to Calcutta with Allen Ginsberg, but now we had come to a parting of the ways. We sat at tea in the lobby of the Imperial and Allen said: *Calcutta makes you make up your mind. There are two things you can do. You can give away what you have and join them on the streets, or you can step over them and make them invisible. Me, I am going to join them.*

We shook hands, and I later heard that Allen had volunteered to burn corpses on the ghats stretching out into the Ganges. I did not "join" them, but neither did they become invisible. How could one ignore them?

Looking from my window at the Imperial, I saw dozens lying on the pavement outside—the homeless, preparing for sleep. It was a very cold evening, and during the night the cold deepened. In the morning I looked at the pavement below. Many of the homeless were awake, moving away. A few still slept. After my breakfast I looked again from the window. The ambulances were removing what I had thought were late sleepers. They were the dead.

Looking from my curtained window of the Imperial I saw the future of us all. Calcutta, Delhi, Mumbai—these are now what London, Paris, New York will eventually become, when further billions are born and have nowhere to go.

India is not only the past. It is also the future.

*

At Khajuraho, that ecstatic celebration of the very vitality that now crowds the earth. Temples carved with loving couples, hundreds of niches in which stand copulating pairs. They stand like open-windowed apartment houses, with all their privacy exposed to the public stare.

And celebrated—Khajuraho is so full-frontal that it is more proclaiming than exhibiting. It does not seek to excite but to enthuse, to enliven. While it can be read as an enormous how-to series of stone-cut frescoes, it is also a demonstration of a universal urge, a compulsion that knows no borders. We of the West may wander India and wonder at the meaning of this or that, but in Khajuraho there is no possibility of our mistaking the purport of these carvings.

Nor the spirit in which they are offered. These demigods are already halfway into immortality. They are real flesh already turned to solid stone yet still retaining its lovely curved humanity. They stand on the lintel of freedom, that transformation into the ineffable.

They still smile and gaze at us, but they are already far distant. Self as they knew it is lost as freedom from self is gained.

And as we stare at these bodies turning in their niches, climbing to the sky, we understand what they are showing us.

Freedom from self is to be gained in many ways—concentration, meditation, the emptying of the mind, the suspension of thought. But the way we all know, and practice, the lingua franca, is the ritual of having sex. Here the self is left far behind as free mind races toward ecstasy.

We climax, we are anonymous, our worldly burden is lifted. It is like a leap upward, a reaching, a heart-pounding effort to become something we are not yet. But something we will be—unified.

This is what these myriads of figures are doing as well. They have relinquished the self and discovered a myriad identity. Though the spectacle may now embarrass the Western-educated Indian—as may too close a study of the *Bhagavad-Gita*, the classic text of Hinduism—the writhing figures at Khajuraho are not only erotic, they are also symbolic.

The place is full of flowers, and this is as it should be because Khajuraho is itself full of a like display. What are blossoms but genitals?—the stamen, the pistils. An open flower offers a mirror of copulation.

And now this beautiful, irresistible urge, this call to leave self and to merge is also responsible for India filling up completely, to be followed by the rest of the world.

BHUTAN

The World As It Used to Be

The first visitors to Bhutan, two monks in the ninth century, called it "the hidden world." And hidden it remained. True, several Portuguese priests arrived (and left) in 1627, but for the next three hundred years further European visitors came only some dozen times. Until 1961 all entry was still by foot or on horseback.

The small (about the same size as Switzerland) country is a part of that gigantic escarpment that rises from the plains of India and continues on up to the plateau of Tibet. Bhutan has long been separate from the rest of the world.

Flying from Bangkok into the airport at Paro, I see that, even from the air, Bhutan is different. We fly over miles of natural forest, and the rivers are wide and undammed. There is no industrial haze, and the land is farmed in small, neat, personal plots.

It seems an untouched Himalayan land. The light is as clear as the air in this kingdom, and sunshine and shade are so differentiated that they seem like two different countries. Bhutan is high (Thimpu, the capital, has an elevation of 6,000 feet; Paro is 7,000 feet), pressed against a sky so blue it seems black.

This far up in the mountains, during the winter the

weather fluctuates. It can be warm enough of an afternoon to walk about in a sweater. When evening comes (or when the sun goes), however, be prepared with layers more, for it gets very cold—in Thimpu in December a maximum in the lower 70s (F) to a minimum of mid-30s.

Immigration is a desk and a smiling man in a sash and robe who stamps the passport and takes the $20 (U.S.), and the airport itself is a pleasantly proportioned wooden house with a number of animals tethered nearby. I am no longer in the modern world. This is what the eighteenth century would have been like had there been airplanes.

And automobiles. There are now roads cutting through the mountains, the major highway being that between the divided town of Phuntsholing (the Indian name of which is Jaigaon) in the south and Thimpu in the middle of the country.

If one entered Bhutan here, from the south, it would entail a sensational climb past enormous waterfalls and through virgin forests. During this six-hour uphill drive, the trees would change from banyan to birch. Oranges would be for sale in the poinsettia-lined streets in the south, and after only half a day's travel there would be frost, snow, and meat drying in the cold and brilliant sun.

There is another shift as well—a temporal one. As we moved up to the high plateau, we would seem to move backward in time as well. Signs of modernity would be mostly left behind, and the architecture would turn traditional. The people now wear Bhutanese dress—robes folded at the breast, something like kimono but quite short for the men, longer for the women.

As the first patches of snow appear among the cedars and junipers, these kilt-like garments remind of some Himalayan Scotland, an effect heightened by the tartan-like patterns favored mostly by the men. There is a northern feeling, too, in the crisp bite of the air, the evident hardiness of the Bhutanese, those straight, clear gazes used to looking at distant mountain ranges.

*

Though there is an airport, mass tourism is discouraged. One of the three pilots licensed to thread these mountain corridors said that though a Boeing 737 might actually land there, "you couldn't fly it out."

One of the reasons the country feels of another age is that it only "opened," or was made accessible to plane, in 1974, and the changes have as yet been few. What with the "kimono," the curiosity, the decorum, I—who have lived most of my life in Japan—could only think that the early Meiji era must have been something like this. But unlike in Meiji Japan, in Bhutan the outside world has so far been kept in its place.

Tourism changes things, always for the worst. The Bhutanese need only look to their neighbor for proof. Nepal gets about a quarter million tourists a year, while Bhutan still gets only a fraction of that. A result is Katmandu International Airport, big hotels clamoring to be filled, and a cultural invasion that has changed the country forever.

Bhutan, on the other hand, has already turned a quarter of its land into wildlife parks and sanctuaries and has pledged to keep more than half of its landscape forested forever. Hunting is forbidden, and you have to get a license to fish.

And there was, until quite recently, no television. Though Bhutan has access to satellite service, this was wisely used only for international telephone and telegraph service. You saw sets around, but these were used mainly for video cassettes. Without that great leveler, TV, Bhutanese tradition had some chance of surviving, at least for a time.

Also, the King of Bhutan and his civil government have requested his subjects to please wear the native dress, to please build in traditional styles. And he is held is such reverence that his wishes have been granted. Though imported clothing is available, most people prefer their familiar dress—the only concession has been the Indian-made imitation-Adidas footwear that has now everywhere taken the place of traditional felt boots.

There are a few signs for Coca-Cola or Pepsi, but these beverages are merely a part of Indian merchandise being carried up from the plains below. There is no franchising, no McDonald's. Such decisions were arrived at through royal request and/or constitutional discussion.

Though Bhutan is officially a kingdom, it has only been such since 1907 (before that it was theocratic), and the present king, Jigme Singye Wanghuck, is the fourth. Also, the royal government of Bhutan is a constitutional monarchy.

Ideally, decisions are made at the village level and are implemented as they move higher into the governmental bureaucracy. The Tashichodzong, the religious and administrative center of the country, holds the various votes of its representatives—100 from the people, 40 from the government, and 10 from the religious.

The governing is democratic, but this does not mean there are no problems. At present there is a pressing one. Nepali-speaking Hindus now make up a quarter of Bhutan's population and, among other things, protest what they call discriminatory dress, language, and building codes. A move was made to send the more recent arrivals back, and this has resulted in some acrimony.

As in neighboring Tibet—and, of course, India—religion in Bhutan holds a special place. Indeed, it is a special religion, since Bhutan is the only country still practicing the tantric beliefs of the Drukpa sect of Kagyupa Mahayana Buddhism. It is from this sect, incidentally, that the country derives its true name: Druk Yul, the Land of the Thunder Dragon. ("Bhutan" is what neighbors and visitors call the place.)

State and religion not being separated, religious life remains decisive. There are numbers of temples, and it is customary (though not compulsory) that one of the sons in a family go through training as a monk. Indeed, becoming a monk is still (in contrast to most Asian countries now) a great honor in Bhutan. .

Most of the 600,000 people in Bhutan (some eighty-five percent) are farmers, and in the fairly recently established (1953) capital of Thimpu there are still only 30,000 citizens. The great diaspora from country to city so common in other countries has not occurred. The average wage per month in Bhutan is 4,000 *nu*—a little over $100 U.S.

It is all of these factors—and the architecture—that make the country feel it is from another time. Bhutan is still a land of very small communities, a few families and their neighbors; several homes around a cross-road; mountain hamlets—all electrified only in 1986.

The common farmhouse is traditional: three stories, with animals on the ground floor, the family on the second, and on the third (open, the roof held only by pillars) a drying space for fodder. The construction is a combination of field stones with wood-inlaid window niches, originally done without plans or nails—an elementary but elegant design. The only modern innovation is that the slate roof being difficult, corrugated iron is (however unfortunately) used.

The food staple is rice (the Bhutanese eat more than two pounds a day), and along with it are various stews (some quite heavily spiced), yak meat (very tender), *datsi*, a soft local yak cheese. There is also the Tibetan dumplings, *momos*. A famous beverage is buttered tea. More like a soup (tea, salt, butter, churned together), it is often drunk, accompanied by such snacks as *zao* (toasted rice), *sip* (flattened rice), and *pchie* (roasted flour). Naturally, in this part of the world, the tourist drinks bottled water. But there is also (Indian) beer, and a variety of other drinks.

The many fortresses (for Tibet often tried to conquer Bhutan), called *dzong*, are strongly built, thick-walled, and quite castle-like. They give the country its high Himalayan air, which has inspired some tourists to call it a "little Tibet."

Anxious to escape the fate of big Tibet, Bhutan closed its borders to that country (and consequently to China) in 1959, and from 1960 began examining ties with India. The impetus may have been the fate of a neighboring country, Sikkim. Presented with a similar dilemma, Sikkim chose India—and is now one of that country's provinces. Bhutan has made a wiser choice and is now a member of the United Nations, an organization that can perhaps be counted upon to protest annexations.

Though Bhutan was never successfully invaded and was never colonized, its people come from various ethnic strains: In the east, a portion of the country still relatively isolated (nine hours by car from Thimpu), the people are the native Sharchops; otherwise the population is Ngalop, descendants of Tibetans who long ago came to the country, and the Nepalese who live largely in the south and arrived not so long ago.

All speak a common language, *dzongkha,* a dialect similar to Tibetan, though now there is another shared tongue as well: English has been designated the principal medium of instruction in public schools since the 1960s. Education is free, right down to the paper and pencils, and there is now a new university. All medical service is also free, including treatment abroad. And this in a land where almost everyone still spins prayer wheels.

These various temporal layers make for the distinctive paradoxes of the place. People wearing clothes from a different age ride around in Hondas, monks send holy scripture through e-mail, robed school children living in newly-built medieval homes chat with one another (and with you) in English.

The seemingly fabulous exists as well. In the Paro valley stand great red temples—structures smaller than but as awe-inspiring as the mighty Potala in Lhasa. One such is the Rinpung Dzong, with its covered bridge, and above it the Ta Dzong, a fortress that is now the national museum.

On the way there, clinging to cliffs, is the Tiger's Nest Monastery, the Taktsan, a collection of white temples that hang like swallows' nests, growing out of the mountainside. And in the mountain groves below, one may still see the golden *takin*.

This large bovine mammal, found only in Druk, has the face of a buffalo and the hooves of a moose, and the males are covered with a mottled golden fleece—the females are more gray. It grazes on hardy mountain bamboo and turns its wide-eyed gaze at the intruder as though it knows that it is the national animal of the country.

Legend says it was created by the ancient hero Drukpa Kunley. This tantric master was asked to make a new beast. Out of a heap of animal bones, he constructed the first takin, putting the head of a goat on the body of a cow.

I saw one. Outside Thimpu in the mountains is where a former king had a private zoo. Since zoos are against good Buddhist principles, it was shortly disbanded. Yet even now the once-captive takins and their descendents return to graze. I was sitting in the morning sun gazing at the vale of Thimpu below me, smoke from the breakfast fires mingling with the last mist, the cold night meeting the warm day, and there it was before me, looking at me with its oddly human face—this golden creature from the hidden world.

What if I were to live here? This is an option offered the tourist—to become an expatriate. To be sure, I already am one, having spent my life in a land (Japan) other than that in which I was born (the USA). But the nature of expatriation is such that repetitions are possible. Your surroundings can change around you as naturally as do the seasons.

The only problem is that of choice. I must choose some-place I like more than Japan. So far I have considered Greece and Morocco. Now I contemplate Bhutan. And as I board my flight at Paras, I think of common film-fed fanta-sies—the flight from Shangri-la, tears coursing down Ronald Coleman's cheeks.

.

MONGOLIA

Land of Yesterday and Tomorrow

Three times the size of France, twice that of Texas, Mongolia lies between China and Russia, traditionally an uncomfortable position, subjected as it is to the blandishments and deprivations of both of its neighbors. This was not always so. In the twelfth century the Mongol empire extended to Moscow and Baghdad, to Lhasa, to Korea — and all the land in between.

In modern times, however, Mongolia was until recently under the suzerainty of the Soviet Union. Now it fears a Chinese economic and political influence, which could prove overwhelming. Already Mongolia's cashmere industry has been much damaged by Chinese traders, and last year China accounted for more than a third of Mongolian direct investment. Neighbors are quick to offer door-opening aid. Signs at bridges and along roads indicate that the funds came from elsewhere — China, Korea, even Japan. This may make urban Mongolia appear pleasantly international, but it also indicates the coming danger of development.

When a country is developed it is always over-developed, because there are no limits on this kind of advance. It obliterates what it feeds upon. When this occurs in Mongolia it will be a great loss, because this country is still one of the most natural and consequently one of the most beautiful.

✿

Once outside the capital and into the steppes, intrinsic magnificence becomes apparent. Since Mongolia is fairly high (some 5,000 feet in the flatter part of the countryside) the sky is often a deep cobalt blue. Against this stand the other colors—tan, ocher, shale gray, lichen green—watercolor shades in this rolling landscape. With trees growing usually only around water courses, the landscape looks like a grassy desert, with the verdant dune-like hills stretching into the far distance.

And, as in the desert countries, daytime may be warm but the nights are cool—a difference of some 90°F in a single day is not unusual. Mongolia can be 104°F in the summer and –50°C in the winter. Blankets are still necessary on an August night.

Between these extremes is a natural land, one seemingly untouched. There are fish crowding the streams—trout, pike, perch—and animals fill the landscapes—not only such familiar beasts as horses, cows, sheep yaks, and camels, but also boar, deer, bear, sable, foxes, wolves, and lots of marmots.

Mongolia does not, in fact, even now, feel domesticated. Nomad families, tents packed and folded on the backs of their beasts, wander off to better pastures. When they pass it is as though no one has ever been there, as though we are the first to come to this lovely land.

The earth seems folded, heaped with low hills, broken

with enormous crowns of rock, great stones stacked one on another, each with its skirt of conifers. And it does not feel Asian. It is more northern, more elemental—it has something like the beauty of the Scottish highlands with its miles of rock-pierced billiard-green. But here the land is so much larger. It seems to go on forever, these rolling flanks, these steep rock fists.

This is why it also looks so powerfully, so nostalgically like the past. Watching the slowly moving herds, the nomads following, seeing the shadow of the clouds pass across the grassy plains, I feel I am looking into some earlier century. Five hundred years ago must have looked like this. No billboards, no advertisements this far out into the countryside, no power lines, no airplanes, just a simple road and then hundreds of leagues of grassy hills with no one on them.

All the people I see are on the move. The white felt tent (called a *ger*—no longer called a *yurt*, a Russo-Turkish word) is planted for a season and then folded up again. The nomads (who still make up half the population of the country) feed their horses and then they milk their mares and drink the milk (it tastes like bovine skimmed milk), or they invent side jobs. We pass herding people also selling heaps of dried sheepskin, or bottles filled with freshly picked blueberries, cranberries, wild strawberries.

Invited into a ger, I sit with three small children, their mother, and their grandfather, and am given the traditional hospitality of these nomadic people. One by one the plates appear. A kind of breaded dumpling, *boortsog*; squares of curd, called *aaruul*; bowls of *tarag*, which is yogurt; and a silver beaker of the highly alcoholic *shimiin arkhi,* cousin to vodka.

Amazing, this hospitality, for Mongolia is, by any standard, among the poorest of countries. I don't know what the wealthier make, but I'm told that a high-school teacher gets about $100 U.S. a month, and the minimum wage (day laborers, part-timers) is half of that. There is also unemployment, particularly at the upper end, for people over-qualified for the work that is available.

This happens perhaps because there are over 150 institutions that call themselves universities in Ulaanbaatar, the capital, and it is said some 60,000 students graduate to a dearth of job opportunities. And yet this long and vigorous tradition of hospitality.

I do not know that the Mongolians are this hospitable to one another. Perhaps, as in Greece, the honorable tradition of hospitality extends mainly to strangers. But I do know that, as a foreigner, I was treated uncommonly well.

For example, I much wanted to see Mongolian wrestling, but I had missed the annual Naadam festival, which seems to consist of little else. Then I heard that the wrestling pavilion in the center of the city would be staging bouts. Then I learned that all tickets were sold out. Nonetheless, upon expression of my desire, rules were bent, tickets were produced, and there I was in the front row for the event.

❃

Mongolian wrestling is reminiscent of sumo—indeed, it is a probable ancestor. Considered one of the three "manly" sports—the other two are archery and horse racing—it consists of two stout men trying to push each other over. It is, however, much more colorful than the Japanese sport. There is constant ceremonial music, dances imitating eagles and the like; the costumes are tighter and brighter, with little vests and an off-the-shoulder effect; the bodies themselves are different (strong, apparent muscles under taut, pliant skin); and the bouts are both more protracted and more violent than in sumo. There is also open betting in the stands and a feeling of fun—which the stately sumo has now all but eradicated.

A daylong affair, the Mongolian wrestling tournament consists of many seven-round bouts, and the day I saw it the grand prize was given to Sumiyabaazar, younger brother of Dagvador, better known as Asashiro, the sumo champion. "Sumiya" is an obvious favorite—the crowd enthusiastically, unanimously cheered.

✻

To look at a Mongolian crowd is to see a bunch of people getting along together. Though the throng at the wrestling pavilion was enormous and the assemblage outside even more dense, there was a feeling of intimacy that suggested family much more than mere mass.

People push their way through other people, individuals turn to talk to apparent strangers, cars honk in friendly fashion and plow on through. The anonymous circumspection of the Japanese crowd, the impatience of the Chinese, is nowhere to be seen. All of these Mongolian people seem in some way related to one another.

Perhaps this is why the capital is so reassuring. It does not feel like a city of a million or so—half the population of the country. Rather, it feels like a town or even a large village. Nor does Ulaanbaatar (one word, it was the Russians that broke it into two) look Asian. Rather, as it is closer to Siberia than it is to China and has a long history closely entwined with that of its northern neighbor, its colors are Russian colors: tan, brown, gray, winter colors in this late summer, broken by the St. Petersburg blue of a lintel, a door, or the whole front of a house.

There are also small wild spaces between the buildings — either gardens or empty lots; lots of houses that look like dachas; big, grand Moscow-like expanses, such as Sükhbaatar Square; ceremonial structures in the Soviet wedding-cake style; an occasional example of East European modernism — the bold, jagged Chinggis Khaan Hotel, designed by a Yugoslavian architect back when there was a Yugoslavia. But with it all is an attractive messiness, an unselfconscious disarray indicating that civic endeavor has a low priority.

Privatization is a growing fact in modern Mongolia. There are joint ventures (with Japan as well as Russia and China), an unwieldy bureaucracy is being slowly whittled away, and individual businesses are appearing everywhere. Farming, for example, is not collectivized, and produce is produced as needed. This means that vegetables are now everywhere available, and that fresh fruit (expensive, since brought from China) is sold on street corners.

But urban sprawl is also a fact — it's one of the reasons for the attractively messy aspect of the capital. Along with the permanent Russian-style buildings, which give the city its Siberian look, there are also whole imbedded ger settlements, towns of traditional tents. These round, felt structures, each with its own chimney, seem at home on the steppes that make up most of Mongolia but, packed into the no-longer-nomadic city, they may enhance the pleasingly semi-permanent aspect of the place, but they aren't very practical in what is, after all, a large and growing urban center.

There is some attempt to preserve native Mongolian culture, and an even stronger impulse to cash in on it. Traditional cashmere is still carded and knitted into luxurious garments, available here at a tenth of the price they bring abroad. The enchanting music of Mongolia (including the astonishing delight of *khoom*—or "throat singing") is preserved and performed by ensembles that now have their own theater. Religion (Tibetan Buddhism or Lamaist), after enduring terrible purges from the 1920s on, has returned. Around 150 new monasteries have been opened, and Ulaanbaatar's largest temple-compound, the Gandan Khiid (never officially closed, kept open as a "museum" of the "feudal period"), is daily thronged.

Commercial interests also drive this modest retro boom. There are several "Mongolia Lands" in the suburbs of the capital. The one I went to had young men employed to stalk around in medieval costumes and have their pictures taken with the tourists, foreign and Mongolian alike. In the main ger we were seated on thrones, ate with silver, and were served a salad of potatoes and cucumbers, something called *harshil* ("black soup") which turned out to be bouillon, fried battered beef cutlets, and, incongruously, chocolate ice cream. The meal was dignified by being called The Ghinggis Khaan Special (not "Genghis Khan," that is a Persian spelling) and included a trip to the gift shop.

❁

There is now, everywhere in the world, in every museum, at every historical site, the emporium where you may purchase some putative part of the imperiled past. Not that these are real artifacts—they are plainly imitations and are sold as such: dull machine-made "Mongol" knives, woven "snow leopard" hats, "Chinese" scarves, rayon masquerading as silk. And there, in a corner, as though admitting fraud, candidly sits a stuffed Mickey Mouse.

Claude Lévi-Strauss writes of civilizations past their peak but perhaps on their way to another. All that is left is a small patch, like snow in the sun. From being eternal it has become historical. Yet even here, in the Mongoland Store, something remains.

One of the Mongol guards sauntering around in full costume speaks English. He learned it at school and likes to practice with the tourists.

"Spring will come," he says, and I think he is perhaps quoting something but he looks at me so earnestly that I agree. "Then I will go home," he adds.

His is a part-time job. He is an ancient Mongol only during fall and winter. In spring and summer he is a modern Mongol.

"I will go back home and help with the ger and get the horses ready and then we start," he says.

He and his family are nomads—herding the horses from one grassy field to the next, just as the ancient Mongols did. This has been going on for a long time, this continuity. But for how much longer, I wonder.

I read that recently Mongolian Prime Minister Tsakhiagiyn Elbegdorj said: "China is becoming sort of an empire. We hope they can become a responsible empire." And he added: "We have no intent to hurt other countries, and we expect the same from our neighbors." This indicates a general feeling that Mongolia is not entirely in control of its future. Too much depends on its neighbors. Mongolia had long and deep connections with Tibet, and it can now see what has happened to that country. It has been obliterated—it is now a province of China. There is no more Tibet. Tomorrow's Mongolia might be no different.

CHINA

Inside the Forbidden City

"But the multitudes are so vast, their numbers have no end. The courts would still have to be crossed, and after the courts the second outer palace, and once more stairs and courts . . . and so on for thousands of years."

Thus wrote Franz Kafka, imagining an imperial messenger attempting to find his way through the Zijincheng, the Forbidden City. This mammoth maze, where it was said "even water turns to jade within these marble banks," stands at the center of the world. Nine thousand rooms spread over 183 acres, capital of rulers for nearly five hundred years, from 1420 to 1911, this Forbidden City, the Imperial Palace, indicates within its very structure a rigid ethical structure, that of *feng shui*, the magical science of geomancy.

This imperial palace is laid out upon a precise north-south axis, and all the many structures within it conform to the natural good fortune inherent in the land. Gates are shut to keep it from running out; others are open to let it run in. There is a bad direction, the southwest, and nothing is there but forbidding towers and guardian dragons. Some say even the imperial sewers conform to feng shui.

Kafka's imperial messenger was racing not only along lacquered corridors and through marble courts. He was also swiftly tracing the invisible lines that control right and wrong, good fortune and bad.

"This city within a city," wrote David Kidd, who knew old Beijing well, "has been the unmoving purple polestar, the heaven-and-earth-touching vertical axis around which the whole earth turned. Seated in state, the emperor faced due south along the central horizontal axis of the city, arched over by a series of monumental gates, the sacrosanct meridian through which imperial power reached out to all of China and, from there, the world."

This geometry, harmony over diversity, symmetry without repetition, has been extraordinarily imposed — as though balance alone could remedy the inchoate, as though a truly colossal chaos had itself occasioned and made necessary this most severe of remedies: the Forbidden City.

The Communist Party apparently thought so, and in its own way observed feng shui. When it came into power, workmen were put to digging right in front of the Gate of Heavenly Peace, right at the operative end of the "sacrosanct meridian." This is where they planted the flagpole that would carry the banner of the Peoples' Republic. The choice of location is interesting — as though the Communists were tapping into half a millennium of imperial good fortune.

Perhaps similar considerations saved the Forbidden City itself. Originally the Communist Party intended to tear it down and construct modern government buildings. But something else prevailed — "good fortune," perhaps.

The peaceful hordes now crowding the once-forbidden city certainly seem pleased to be within these once-sacred geomantic precincts. Streaming crowds of people — Chinese common people—come to stare, to spill into the gardens, to thumb the lacquer and finger the filigree. They wander the corridors, the courts, and the endless rooms of the museums that, together, hold the "more than 900,000 pieces." They stare at the bronze lion-dogs—the big ones crushing the little ones—which in turn stare defiantly into the southwest. And there the visitors sit, these thousands, exhausted by this stunning immensity, this wilderness of marble terraces and stairs, this forest of red lacquer pillars, this incredible landscape of a palace.

One of the best descriptions of the place was written by a displaced Frenchman, Victor Segalen, whose hero in the novel *René Leys* was obsessed by the Forbidden City. "I encircle it, dominate it, square my eye to its form: I comprehend it. The buildings, the courtyards, the open spaces, the different palaces of the Palace are all there, laid out with schematic symmetry like the cells of a honey-comb . . . four hundred million men gathered hereabout, differing no more among themselves than the workers of the hive, agglomerated these chessboard squares, these straight, sharp forms, these cells . . ."

There is a route through it. Traditionally one entered the Meridian Gate in the south. Nowadays one goes through the Central Arch, formerly reserved for the emperor. Beyond lies the Golden Stream, where water turns to jade; the Gate of Supreme Harmony, where the lion-dogs raise their paws.

Up, through the gate, and one is at the Sea of Flagstones, where it is said that 90,000 can stand and presumably have. (Somewhat less than that number stood there for those several scenes actually filmed in the Forbidden City for *The Last*

Emperor.) Beyond is the largest and grandest of the imperial structures, the Hall of Supreme Harmony, among the treasures of which are the Nine-Dragon Screen and the musical Chimes of Jade.

Up to the Hall of Complete Harmony, then on to the Hall of Preserving Harmony, then down to the Dragon Pavement, carved marble said to weigh two hundred tons; then more halls, more gates, on and on. All have sternly ethical names — Supreme Harmony, Heavenly Purity, Earthly Peace, Divine Prowess. These grand abstract virtues are like the right-angled orientation, the metaphorical axis, the feng shui symmetry. They make one wonder what threat made all of this necessary. In China, was chaos this large?

Apparently so. Beneath the pure ostentation of the place, the sheer conspicuous consumption, is the roar of the inchoate, the immemorial ferment of China. A stern balance of doctrine must hold these blind forces in check.

Yes, I read in the morning paper that some villagers went and stole some watermelons. Then I read on and discover that the culprit villagers number 2,000. How does one contain 2,000 sudden offenders against law and order? One does not. They can only represent a leak in the massive dike of which both the Forbidden Palace and the Communist Party are parts.

The masses, then, perch on the marble and stare, impressed by all this magnificence, which has but one end — to impress them. There are no Mao caps around now (well, one, on a visiting village child), and everyone is dressed in Third World American: T-shirt, something like jeans, and a few flashes of fashion — this summer, black plastic Panama hats on flaming youth. Yet now, at the Forbidden City, they gape as they always have, as though at a natural wonder.

I do not know if anyone knows history any longer, and so I cannot guess if they might be thinking of processions of crimson and purple, of courts filled with courtiers, of the intrigues of eunuchs. When I see a farm family inspecting the well in which the lovely Pearl Concubine was drowned, I do not know what they might be seeing.

In small chambers in the Summer Palace, people dress up to get photographed. The sweating farmer's wife giggles and struggles with the heavy brocaded robes of a Qing court dress. The headdress is lowered over her slippery brow. She is invited to turn and look at the waiting Empress Dowager, a waxen figure likewise bedecked.

Flash! And here one may divine what the farmer's wife is thinking. She is dressing up; she wants to her picture taken in good surroundings, among a better sort of people. One wonders, however, at the Communist government's apparently also wanting this.

After wandering with the crowds through the halls and palaces, the side corridors with their multitude of chambers, I finally, at the far north, find the imperial gardens, all gnarled stones, gazebos, carp ponds, the concubine's unhappy well.

Here the multitudes collect, grateful for green shade after the blinding marble and the blazing crimson lacquer. Unlike in Kafka's vision, reality does finally make an end of this gigantic piece of geomancy, the very weight of which irons out differences to create constants of time and space, of north and south, of good fortune and bad. For the time being.

Once finally outside, I am suddenly again aware of chaos.

It takes the form of noise—ordinary, deafening Chinese noise. These are the people who invented the Beijing opera, all gongs and cymbals and piercing falsetto. Their language makes its users sound angry, as though they are shouting at one another. It is the land of the loudspeaker. And, of course, the Chinese invented fireworks.

Inside the Forbidden City these same now-liberated throngs are quiet. There is silence, as though the weight of the place had suppressed all natural noise. Outside, no such constraint. Order is unimposed, and humanity begins again to bubble.

My taxi driver is unhappy with me. I have requested that he turn off, or at least lower the volume of, his deafening tape of American rock. Then I think, why not? Rock, with its sheer decibel level, its tinny amplification, its sound of a cheap radio played far too loud, is the real music of China. Here is the deafening vitality of these people. Perhaps the quiet hordes at the Forbidden City were merely awed at their own silence.

LAOS

The Old Capital of Luang Prabang

In the early years of the last century, the wife of a French colonial doctor wrote in her journal: "Oh! What a delightful paradise. The fierce barrier of the stream protects this country from the progress and ambition of which it has no need. Will Luang Prabang be, in our century of exact sciences, of quick profits, of victory by money, the refuge of the last dreamers?"

Yes, is the answer, nearly a hundred years later.

Paradises do rest upon the past, and they last only so long as progress is kept at bay. So far, development, investment, exploitation have been successfully resisted. Or perhaps it is just that Laos is late in joining the rest of the progressive nations.

The country was reopened to tourists in 1989, and its ancient capital, Luang Prabang, was rendered generally accessible only ten years later, when the new flight, Bangkok–Luang Prabang, was initiated. Progress—development, the tourist industry—has consequently not yet completely had its way.

Another deterrent is that the old capital was in 1995 declared by UNESCO to be a World Heritage site—the best preserved city in what used to be called Indochina. There

$_s$ higher than a coconut tree, origi-
nes when invaders forced the removal
ntiane) are to be preserved, as are the

nth century someone counted them and dis-
ve. Today nearly half of these temples, thirty-
tv.   still in operation—an indication that Buddhist
traditio.   rives. As it should, since the city's name, I was
told, means Great (Luang) Buddha (Prabang.) Indeed, the
place often seems a city of monks. Of the some 15,000 inhabitants, hundreds are yellow-robed boys and young men.

Their rounds start at five in the morning, as they walk the
streets receiving alms, a daily ritual called *takbaat*. One sees
them everywhere, coming and going, creating an odd feeling
of timelessness.

The magnificent Wat Xieng Thong (Golden City Monastery), built in 1560, seems to look as it always has. Roofs
sweep low to the ground in Lao fashion, ancient bodhi trees
spring from the temple pavements, royal gold shines against
peasant pinks and blues, dusty statues are stacked in dim re-
cesses—as though waiting. It could be a century earlier.

Equally traditional are the markets, open from five in the
morning to five in the afternoon. One is for household goods,
and the other is for food. To arrive when the latter opens and
by candlelight view the ruby-red blood pudding, the golden
chicken-feet, the great clumps of basil and coriander, is to
understand what life was like in the past, to comprehend the
enormous power of continuity.

Secluded in the forested, mountainous regions of the
north, protected by the barrier of the Mekong River, the

city was always considered difficult to reach and was hence spared the full weight of colonization. A French civil servant in the 1930s noted that it took longer to travel by river from Saigon to Luang Prabang than it did to travel by sea from Marseilles to Saigon.

One result of this seclusion is that the city has been allowed to go its own way. While Vientiane is rapidly modernizing (the Lao People's Democratic Republic is, after all, now a member of the powerful ASEAN—Association of Southeast Asian Nation—trading group) the provinces remain as they were.

Another factor favoring tradition is the mellowing of governmental policy. After the "revolution" of 1975 and the taking over of the country, the Communist Pathet Lao prohibitions against Buddhism were ignored to the extent that they were soon dropped. As early as 1979 the government began loosening what has since been called the straitjacket of Stalinist economics—particularly, it backed down from the highly unpopular policy of agricultural collectivism.

At the same time, the government began to look to the past and to allow and even sponsor an official version of it. Symptomatic is the elevation of the last king of Laos, Sisavang Vong, who died in 1959. Visits to the newly restored and now completely ostentatious royal palace are suggested. There I am shown various relics—presents from other foreign heads of state, an oil portrait (Russian), a bronze statue (Russian)—and encouraged to regard royal rule in a favorable manner one would have thought impossible in a communist country.

As yet there is almost no mention of the king's son, who

ascended the throne upon his father's death. According to official Pathet Lao history, the 1975 "revolution" prevented the actual coronation. There is another version, however. After serving as "adviser" to the president, King (or Crown Prince) Sisavang Vatthana—a cultured man who (among other accomplishments) read Proust—and his family were exiled to the north. There they eventually expired, one by one it is said; starved, it is alleged, in a cave.

However, there is another version of this story. An official brochure says that the Proust-reading king returned and generously offered his palace to the government. This would indicate that he is still living in Luang Prabang, but I met no one who had ever seen him. His father, however, is not so neglected. His spirit is very much there, in the golden palace, indicating what a glorious past the present has.

And indeed, the government has instituted a number of reforms. It now allows farmers to own their land and to sell their crops at market prices. Trade, banking systems, foreign investment have all been, to an extent, liberalized. Economic problems (which, to be sure, keep the place, from this tourist's point of view, "paradisiacal") remain. The country is very poor, and it is also underpopulated.

Though Laos is about the same size as Britain, its population—some five million—is only eight percent of the British population. There are reasons. At the time of the Communist takeover some ten percent of the population, including many of the country's commercial and administrative experts and skilled technicians, fled. Included in this diaspora were also some three-quarters of the intelligentsia and the overseas-educated.

In addition, Laos was attacked. The U.S. carpet-bombed strategic areas of the country during the late 1960s and early 1970s, and people were killed in these bombings. Places such as Nambak were heavily hit, but Luang Prabang, in the same province, was relatively spared. Still, I saw spent U.S. shell casings used as planters and a U.S. parachute serving as a wedding pavilion.

Though the Lao Lum, the lowlanders, still form about fifty percent of the population, Laos has more minority groups—the government estimates some sixty-eight—than any of its neighbors. These, the so-called "hill tribes," are far removed from progressive Vientiane.

There has been a good deal of governmental persuasion to have these people moved to the lowlands. They can there be better integrated, and a watch can be kept on what they grow, since some cultivate the beautiful, lucrative, and dangerous poppy.

Around the outskirts of Luang Prabang there are now a number of former hill-tribe settlements. The Khamus are much in evidence, but the most numerous are members of the Hmong tribe. I went to a village outside the town and saw many traditional homes, all made of natural materials, each containing a loom, since the Hmong are among the finest of the local weavers.

And in the midst of these homes was a new one—pure Palm Springs—made of concrete, with gables, a front door, glass windows, a porch. The owner, I was told, had a lot of money—because he had relatives in America.

Indeed, the United States hosts a large Hmong colony. This is because, during the 1960s, a number of Hmong people were recruited by the CIA to fight both North Vietnamese and Laotian communists. When these took over Laos, the Hmong went into refugee camps, and hundreds of thousands, it is said, eventually settled in the United States.

The majority left in Laos, however, do not yet build with concrete. Indeed, their contact with modern civilization is minimal. I went to see one of the traditional Hmong celebrations. This was a seasonal get-together, when the young people, dressed in their finest, gathered in a nearby grove to engage in what looked like a ritual sport but was really a mating game.

As the two lines of youngsters, boys on one side, girls on the other, tossed small winter oranges back and forth, they sang traditional songs and at the same time sized one another up. The girls were demure and aloof but making the most of their elaborate costumes. The boys were, in salesman-like fashion, enumerating their own finer points.

And at one side were some older people, pencils poised, tape recorders running, who were transcribing these old songs. Walkman in ear, others were checking the various versions.

This startling sight was, I thought, a metaphor for modern Laos. Monks use pocket calculators, deep-dish TV antennae bring the world into the living room, rock booms just around the corner, and here medieval courtship dances are unselfconsciously being performed in a sylvan grove.

Those of us who approve of paradises and court nostalgia must always face the awkward fact that life is better for people once paradise passes. Here, however, is one way to retain it. Laos takes what it wants of the new, retains what it will of the old, and in the amalgam holds much of what is useful and beautiful of the past while reaching into the future.

CAMBODIA

The Other Treasures of Angkor

Cambodia's Angkor is an enormous site located on a wooded plain where, between the ninth and the fourteenth centuries, the Khmers built this spectacular administrative and religious center. Here, the early kings ruled over a vast territory, which extended from what is now Vietnam across to the Bay of Bengal, and up into China as far as Yunnan. Remaining after the collapse of the Khmers are nearly three hundred temples and palaces, some thirty of which have been cleared of forest and may be visited.

The most famous of these is the major remaining structure, Angkor Wat—that huge compound that is one of the wonders of the ancient world. But around it, though often at some distance, are many other sites that are often just as interesting and occasionally even more beautiful.

*

Angkor Thom, an area of six square miles, is a fortified city, once completely walled and with a wide moat said to have been stocked with crocodiles. Five great guarded gates led into it, and these have more or less survived for eight centuries. The gates are crowned with four gargantuan faces of the bodhisattva Avalokiteshvar, each facing a cardinal direction.

This bodhisattva is even more thoroughly there in the Bayon, an inner monument comprising fifty-four towers decorated with his giant visage—some two hundred faces in all. The expression is enigmatic—some have seen only eyes watching, some have seen the famous Khmer smile.

Paul Claudel, French ambassador in the 1920s, found merely "evil," but many (including, presumably, its builder, Jayavarman VII) saw only the infinite compassion associated with Buddhism—the then-new religion that contended for a time with the native Hindu until amalgamating with it.

※

Clambering over the ruins (the Bayon is much less reconstructed than Angkor Wat), wandering through the long corridors, climbing the steep stairways, I am continually observed by these giant faces. Wherever I turn I have already been apprehended by an attentive profile, or an almost invisible smile, or just half a countenance, riven by a giant root. Perhaps this seeming surveillance is what Claudel was talking about, though the regard could just as easily be interpreted as benign.

Here is architecture as image. The entire structure can be seen as a mandala, with Buddha in the center. Or an allegory, the faces an assembly of the deities. The Chinese envoy Zhou Daguan, who visited the place in 1296, wrote down what it was like then. The Buddhas were immense, the colonnades and corridors stretched forever, and where the sovereign sat there was a great golden window that opened onto a splendid court. Here "men and women alike are anointed with perfumes compounded of sandalwood, musk and other essences and the worth of the Buddha is universal."

Nonetheless, says Zhou, this vast population was served by slaves, richer families owning more than a hundred. But the economy was in a sound state. So were the morals. His example was that there was no punishment for adultery. If the husband found out, he had the lover's feet squeezed until the pain grew unendurable and he surrendered all his property as the price for liberation.

✻

The royal palace itself has been long swallowed up by the vegetation, and its remains are scattered about the enormous park of Angkor Thom, a ceremonial space filled over the centuries with examples of civic endeavor, many of them still standing.

Here is the Terrace of the Elephants, perhaps a reviewing stand for public ceremonies. I imagined the chariots, the cavalry, the infantry—the flags, pennants, all those carapaced elephants—and what Zhou Daguan describes as a whole forest of ceremonial umbrellas, those with gold handles reserving the highest rank.

Here, too, is the famous Terrace of the Leper King. Perhaps the leprosy was merely the result of later lichen observed on the statue of Yama, god of death (a copy of which is there still in all its stigmata—the original is in Pnom Penh's National Museum), or maybe there really was such an unfortunate ruler. The Japanese novelist Yukio Mishima thought so. He stayed, he said, for hours. Then he returned home and wrote a play about the place, called *The Leper King*.

Perhaps, it is said, the terrace is merely the roof of something else, the touches of disease and death being added because the building on which it rested was the royal crematorium. It is not difficult to believe this. Climbing down the stairs leads you to a winding corridor, narrow, constricting, as though about to strangle—a serpentine lair in the bowels of which one is lost. High above is the slender path of the suddenly distant sky. Here it is easy to think of death, for up ahead there is the music of the damned—a wailing flute. I turn a corner and I see the flautist, a maimed man in the shadows, his cap set optimistically in front of him.

Dotted about the park—so oddly reminiscent of Versailles, another ceremonial showplace—are further temples, palaces. New, these would embody a probably insufferable ostentation—slave labor, bright hues, all that gold. But the color has vanished along with the gold and we are looking at ruins. These we are allowed to find morally consoling—pride has had its fall.

❋

Ta Prohm, not far distant, is Angkor as it was "discovered" by the first French (for people in the neighborhood, of course, Angkor had never been lost)—swallowed by the "jungle," a mighty pile of ruins: crumbling towers, closed courtyards, narrow corridors, the mighty stones pushed by

the roots of the enormous trees, all lined with lichen and car-
peted with moss.

Built at the end of the twelfth century, again by Jayavarman VII, this vast ruin was once home to some 80,000 people, including, say the records, more than 600 dancers. Now it
is filled only with tourists, and — adding to the picturesqueness
of the site — children. These are the guides who will lead you to
the best position from which to take photos and insure against
your becoming lost in the mazes of the place.

(The days of the begging young at Angkor are over. The
children are now well-behaved businesspeople. They sell
guidebooks and postcards, they act as guides, behaving with
dignity and self-respect. Likewise, adult beggars are no more.
I saw just one, and that was in the nearby town of Siam Riep.
The indigent, the maimed, the blind — these have been formed
into bands, small orchestras that play traditional Cambodian
music from pavilions as the tourists tour the sites. After listening to this magical addition to the sorcery of the place, one
is glad to give.)

Ta Prohm is romantic in its ruin, overgrown, towering
trees dappling the fallen stones, sunlight turning black in the
shadows. It is all extravagantly impressive. My small guide,
seeking to augment, tells me that *Lara Croft: Tomb Raider* was
actually filmed here, but even this information could not less-
en the tremendous dignity of the place.

❧

Banteay Srei, much further off (twelve miles from the
Bayon) is earlier (tenth century) and is at the same time best

preserved. A Hindu temple dedicated to Shiva, it is built of a variety of red sandstone that weathers particularly well. Nowhere else in the Angkor complex are the carvings so sharp, so crisp. Pink, stippled with green verdigris, the temple stands as though pristine. If one thinks of the Petit Trianon it is because of this miniature perfection and also because, after the heavy baroque of Angkor Wat and the Bayon, it appears rococo—something refreshingly, even divertingly human among the monolithic aspirations.

Another reason for its freshness is that until relatively recently it was kept off the tourist map by Khmer Rouge activity. But now that this lethal organization has been assimilated (some ex–Khmer Rouge soldiers are now tour guides, I was told), the place is safe. Also, the land mines that accompanied this terrible regime are now, I am advised, removed or exploded, "except along the Thai border."

❖

Kobal Spien, a fifteen-minute drive from Banteay Srei (plus an hour-long mountain climb), is usually in English called "The River of a Thousand Lingas." Once you have made it to the exhausting top, there they are, smallish phallic-shaped stones, lots of them, submerged in the river, right beside a modest waterfall. Obviously the site is Hindu — Buddhism never made much of lingas, and besides there are also to be found images of Vishnu, Rama, Lakshmi, Hanuman, and so on. What they are doing there and why, I never discovered. The interested tourist will decide whether the reward is worth the exertion.

✿

Preah Khan, the "Temple of the Sacred Sword," is in good condition for a structure dedicated in 1191 — a two-story structure at that. The visitor is guided through the West Gate, which was the original back door. The knowledgeable visitor will therefore walk around the Preah Khan, admiring the columned structure from the outside, then entering through the East Gate door. In this way the place can be seen as intended and one may imagine what it must once have been like. More than five hundred Hindu divinities were celebrated there, and during the course of the year there were nearly twenty major festivals requiring teams of thousands just to look after everything. Now it is empty, filled only with the calls of the birds, the noises of the cicadas, the sunlit scamperings of the lizards, and the suffocating greenery.

✿

Preah Neak Pean nearby, actually a part of Preah Khan, is a large square pool at the center of which is a round "island" created by the two encircling naga "snakes" whose intertwined tails give the place its name. It was, until recently, difficult to get to. Then a new road was made, and now the tourists trickle in. Water also once flowed in, through the four large spouts, from four reservoirs at the compass points of the pool itself. It was used for ritual purification rites, and even now during the rainy season it sometimes fills up again and is just as it was.

Nonetheless, my child guide, an attentive 10-year-old,

saw something leap in one of the ponds and shouted to one of the lounging workers. At once the man was in the sacred mud wrestling with a large, stranded catfish, which was shortly seen writhing in his upraised grasp.

He looked like one of the people—fishermen, farmers—on the friezes of the Bayon, and the gulf of a millennium shrank. Under this sudden vision from the past were the timeless thumps and bangs of classical Cambodian music as under their pavilion of thatch the armless, legless, eyeless orchestra played its ageless tunes and I sat on the lip of the pool, rested, and cogitated.

❖

The continual surprise of travel—that exhilarating state of being able to understand every moment something that back home we are lucky to experience once a month. The food is surprising, the houses are surprising, the people are surprising. Nothing is as it was back wherever home is. Curiosity becomes something like a new way of seeing, of hearing, of being. That is, if we do not interpret difference as threat.

Here I am in the sun, in the jungle, looking at ancient lustral geometry, carved in stone forever, and listening to the human spirit, mutilated but resilient, its broken melody no less permanent. Looking and listening like this is something like meeting an unfamiliar self—someone always there but not often let out like this to sit blinking in the sun. We are reunited by all this difference.

It is as though we are again young. And in the Angkor ruins the corridors are so long, the stairs are so steep, the lintels are so high that we are returned to something like babyhood. We crawl around on the floor, we totter to a door, we are always slipping and falling. While frustrating, this is also salutary. Like the very young, we ascertain, detect, discover — we are quick to learn, yearn though we do for a way out of the labyrinth.

Habit dulls, the same thing constantly seen or heard becomes accepted — that is, we become blind and deaf to it. Only the new, the unexpected, can reach us with something of its original freshness, still alive, not yet killed by our traditional regard. In Angkor not only are we reduced in size, we are also returned to that time when everything was fresh and alive, those early years when we did not know the name of anything.

I look about me as I sit by the reservoir and gaze at the ruins. I don't know what anything is called. And not only because I do not know Cambodian. I do not even know the names of these things in English. And since I am ignorant, I can sense possibility. It is like a cool breeze lingering in the jungle heat as though to revive me.

In the meantime my child guide is impatiently pulling me to my feet. We are behind schedule. There is still much to see, and others are waiting.

❈

Ta Som is now being reconstructed by the World Heritage Foundation. A late (thirteenth century) Buddhist temple, it is famous for a single image — the giant visage of Avalokiteshvara riven by a great anaconda-like root of an ancient liep tree. Search as one may, however, it is no longer there. Reconstruction has removed the root and put the face back together again. There are, however, lots of other examples of temple walls, gates, arches slowly disintegrating in the coils of the trees.

Not only do the liep trees force apart the ancient masonry, they also—roots all above ground—often fall during the rainy reason, bringing down whole temple complexes. One side of Ta Som lies scattered like the pieces of a puzzle. Each is now being numbered and then, jigsaw-like, hoisted into a hopeful approximation.

Even reconstructed work is thus threatened. One whole series of chambers, put together in the 1920s, was recently knocked down by falling trees. It was thought that these could be easily put back together by using the records left by the French archeologists. Then it was discovered that these had been destroyed, like so much else, by the Khmer Rouge.

✿

Pre Rup is another pyramid-shaped temple mountain, with five shrines at the top and lines of steep stairways, a ruined Grand Central Station of beige and gray devoted, in this case, to death. The name means "turning the corpse" and refers to a traditional means of cremation. East Mebon is another enormous pile, with maimed elephants in white stone, and pillars like stacked soup plates. Thammanon looks like an abandoned country house (palace though it was), its black and tan façade so severely French seventeenth century that one expects a marble bust of Corneille. One can understand the excitement of the nineteenth-century French. It must have seemed like time travel to them.

And on and on and on the ruins stretch. Each one, among other things, a magnificent monument to futility. Paul Claudel was, indeed, silly in his observation, but it is at the same time impossible not to think of death. It seems in Angkor somehow close. In Egypt it is equally near, but it is somehow sterilized by the dryness, the heat, the distance from our times, its very memorialization. Angkor was not, however—as these things go—all that long ago. Further, the clinical fact thrust at you at once is that Angkor is organic. It is all twisted, writhing roots, as intimate as bowels, everything alive and rotting. Death is dramatized, and you will find it upsetting only if you find death sinister, which you need not.

✻

The Khmer Rouge and its killing fields left only seven million or so people alive in the country. Now, a quarter-century later, my guide tells, there are close to fifteen million, though one million of these are the tourists. This population is poor but surviving. The farmer makes the equivalent of $100 U.S. a month, the shopkeeper maybe $200. My child guide doesn't know how much he makes.

Such sums would not get you very far in the West today, but prices are low in Cambodia. And the native currency is not the preferred one. The tourist comes and goes (at least this one did) without acquiring any Cambodian riels at all, except as small change. U.S. dollars and Thai baht are currencies of choice and will get you everywhere. Indeed, riels are not much wanted and are, with the rate of nearly 4,000 to a dollar, cumbersome to carry about.

Whether dollars or baht, small denominations are necessary (nearly everything seems to cost, somehow, $1) and are used for transportation, without which you see nothing of the place. There are no taxis, only a few Thai tuk-tuks, and the distances are too vast for rented bikes. One consequently climbs on motor bikes and holds onto the driver as he whizzes you to where you want to go and then holds out his hand for his dollar.

This (or an agency hired car) is the way to see the other treasures of Angkor, spread as they are over such a vast space. Even so, it is difficult to comprehend the sheer size of this enormous political, religious, and administrative area. It covers an area roughly that of inner Washington, D.C., another designed and ceremonial city.

Indeed, one of the ways to apprehend Angkor would be to imagine the ruins of the American capital. Ah, there is the dome of the Capitol, still intact and just visible above the forest; some distance away is the exquisite White House, seen through Virginia creeper and much what it always was, a privileged palace; further off is all that remains of the colonnaded Lincoln Memorial with its seated, brooding ruler; and in straight, linear progression (suggesting some early U.S. prowess in sacred geometry), rearing out of the oak and the pine, is that great, inexplicable lingam that we know only by its mysterious name: the Washington Monument.

VIETNAM

North, South, and Middle

Though Vietnam is now politically unified, it remains still—decades later—divided. Hanoi in the north is socialist, Sovietized, poor, nominally virtuous. Saigon (a name that much better suits the nature of the place than the official Ho Chi Minh City) is Americanized, nouveau riche, nominally worldly. The places are so different, they seem not to belong in the same country.

But they do—schizoid Vietnam, a place that indicates that the horrors of regimentation with no freedom might seem somehow equated with the horrors of freedom with no regimentation.

In Hanoi it is still 1976, and the socialist grip seems tight. Lenin stands there in enormous effigy right in front of the Military Museum. There is poverty (thin men jostling for fares in their cyclos, sad old women, hands outstretched, hordes of children with plastic cards indicating they are real orphans and hence deserving), and citizens with the money for the entrance fee are invited to spend their hours of leisure admiring Uncle Ho's rustic abode, his deathbed still sheeted, his books (Lenin) still open on the desk, and, in the nearby mausoleum, Uncle Ho himself on his bier—except for Mondays and Fridays, and two months a year when the corpse is sent to Moscow for maintenance.

In Saigon it is at least 2026 — heavy overpopulation, crowds day and night, the traffic never stopping, winding its way around American-franchise fast fooderies, past shops, everything for sale, most of it American; gangs of youngsters getting in the way, not begging but worse, setting traps for the unwary — jostling, pickpocketing. I saw two of these muggings, both of white foreigners. No matter where you step, someone else gets there before you, and at night the streets become nearly impossible to cross, with the eating, the drinking, the cars, the cyclos, the jostling crowds. Leisure hours seem spent gambling, or entrepreneuring, and only the tourists in this southern city are taken to the Presidential Palace and the War Crimes Museum.

Hanoi has a gray three million in it, Saigon has an over-stuffed six million flashing by on motorbikes. Yet, there are some similarities. The bureaucracy, for example. Atop a native inclination for Confucian bureaucracy (Vietnam was culturally dominated for centuries by China), there is the later layer of Soviet-inspired socialist bureaucracy, and on top of that the more recent American-style "democratic" bureaucracy. Restrictions are found everywhere — the visitor is at once strangled in them, from immigration onward, and getting out of the place is just as time-consuming as getting in.

The residents have more means of coping. In the north there is patience and apathy and getting to know someone who will help. In the south there is already knowing someone and — of course — money. I was told that money would buy anything, and while this is true everywhere it seems even more true in Saigon.

The dichotomies of this top- (or bottom-)heavy country are apparent, but after a time similarities (beyond the national bureaucracy) surface. In the middle of the country one begins to identify things Vietnamese—and not merely Soviet north or American south. In Hue, for example, the old capital, I could see that the country was not urban at all—it was really rural Asia, upheld by an economy that was not based on manufacture and commerce so much as upon naked agriculture. Water buffalos labored, ridden by rural children, and peasants in their peaked hats bent to plant the early spring rice as they would later bend to cut it. Marketing was primitive and markets were mere gatherings of farmers—the superstructure of produce distribution seemed not yet there.

With this, a rural pleasantness, the smiles of a people committed to getting along by choice rather than command, ready to bend a rule or two because the community is small, because they all know one another, and because a rule will be later bent in their favor.

The foreigner—me, the tourist—is not an object for calculated exploitation (the Hanoi beggar child) nor instant economic availability (the Saigon gangboy), but something like a guest. Unguessable to be sure, and irrational, but not made, at least not entirely made, of money. A glass of tea appears and no outstretched palm follows.

A balance is reached in the city of Hoi An, geographically in the very middle of this long peninsula-shaped country, a place that the French, the Japanese, and the Americans all somehow spared. There is an "old" section with narrow streets and roofs that sometimes meet overhead, where something like what Vietnam once was remains.

Cars are banned, river traffic is encouraged, cafés proliferate, and every other building seems to be an art gallery. Yet the place is not yet gentrified. The stores are not yet boutiques. The city is still in local use—unlike Williamsburg in the USA, or Kurashiki in Japan. I ate good local food at an outdoor table by the river, looked at the boats (loaded with mangoes, with cattle, with children), while the life of the town went on around me.

Hoi An is still real. The people in the city still get along with one another. Usually people in rampant bureaucracies do not. Each bureau is intent only upon its own continuation and hence has its own rules. To use a small example: Our passports were taken away from us in Hue and Danang, but not in Saigon or Hanoi. The police were, on the other hand, helpful (tourist-oriented, indeed) in Hue, but in Danang the police set up blockades on the roads to catch the unwary, to stop them, and to collect fines for imaginary offenses. Foreigners are still favorite targets (though I was lucky), because they speak no known tongues and can appeal to no higher authorities.

But some bureaucracies are more sophisticated than others and see that arbitrarily harassing individuals is not eventually rewarding. Air Vietnam still bumps people in the most whimsical manner, but Vietnam tourism has recognized this as counterproductive and will fight for violated rights. As my guide told me when I found that Air Vietnam would not allow me on the Hanoi flight because of an alleged computer mistake: "You'll make it, don't worry. Believe me, this is not

the first time this has happened." He then phoned Hanoi,
Viettourist called Vietair, and I got on and somebody else got
bumped.

Resourceful, pragmatic, devious if it pays, these are the
ways learned by people who have had to learn them. I stood
in the Cham Museum in Da Nang and looked at the remains
of this Indonesian civilization that had taken over the country, then I stood in the Forbidden City in the Citadel of Hue
and looked at the remains of the Chinese civilization that had
taken over the country, then on the streets of Saigon and
looked at the pleasure pavilions of McDonald's and Colonel
Sanders and Häagen-Dazs, where the Americans had taken
over the country. The Vietnamese have had to be resourceful. The wonder is that they have kept their humanity.

And they've also kept (for a time) the extraordinary
beauty of their long, slender country. For how long I do not
know, for this is a country that is going to become quite rich,
unless China takes it again, or unless it strangles itself, or unless Japan gives lessons on how to uglify a place for profit.

Take Ha Long Bay—it is a scenic marvel, as though the
mountains of south China had been drowned in the sea, then
rose, all 3,000 of them, from the depths, each seemingly as tall
as that single sugarloaf in Rio. It is a landscape so astonishing it does not seem of this earth. To cruise in a small boat
through this mountainous maze is to imagine another planet—one filled with a beauty that this one seems otherwise to
have mostly forgotten.

Yet this wonder is to be discovered only at the end of
an exhausting five-hour (seven if by bus) drive over terrible roads, to be met with a couple of hotels and a handful of

eateries. There is no tourist industry overwhelming what it was the tourist came to see. The future holds its luxury hotels and its five-star restaurants, and the small boats will make way for liners, but right now the beauty remains.

It remains there because no one can afford to obscure it. And also perhaps because there is a kind of respect for the land, a feeling for its integrity. And it is this that I might call Vietnamese. It is this that impressed me more than the divided country, the capitals of extremes, the honeycombs of government, and the heedless flow of mere population. At Ha Long, in Hue, in Hoi An I got to see persons, individuals, and I saw them in their environment and began to understand a little.

THAILAND

The Ruins of Sukothai

An enormous park, filled with history and its remains, Sukothai, the first capital, still sprawls across a wooded plain. Scattered with pillars, portals, sitting, standing roofless Buddhas, it is far too large to walk—long grassy distances between the ruins and the lakes and moats to get across or around. There is a kind of tourist trolley, but it doesn't go very far, and a car is possible but doesn't fit the view, so a bike is better.

Pedaling through the heat (it is April—April is the hottest month) is like pedaling through molasses. Even the dragon-flies, hanging here beside me as I pedal by, seem stunned. Still, I consider as I labor, this heat suits this baked land-scape—burned, brown brick reflected in warm green water.

I stop and gaze at the reflection of the biggest Buddha of them all—that inside the Wat Si Chum, all brick and stucco, nearly fifty feet tall. I peer at him through a slit in his temple wall, and detect a sunlit glitter. His fingernails are covered with gold leaf, pressed there by his pilgrims.

Somewhere around in back is supposed to be a passage leading up to his ears—and his mouth. Not only could you pray to him, but he could answer you, thanks to favor-able acoustics and strategically placed monks. One of the

Sukothai kings is supposed to have brought his troops here to listen to the encouragingly bellicose words of the Buddha.

Perhaps that king was Ramkhamhaeng (1278–99), says my guidebook. His father and grandfather had carved the capital out of land long taken by the Khmers, intruders from what is now Cambodia. Now he, the third of Sukothai's kings, not only introduced the alphabet, he also established Buddhism as the common faith.

There is a stele in the local museum (a copy, the original is in Bangkok) that describes the place as a utopian land, plentiful and ruled over by a compassionate monarch. However, like all utopias, this one did not last. By the middle of the fifteenth century it had vanished, and the capital was now far south in Ayutthaya, the ruins here then looking perhaps something like they do now.

I look at the Buddha. In Thailand he has a roundish face and an expression that has been called feline, as though he had just swallowed something good. Also, unlike in some other countries, he is awake, up and about. Indeed, that is the point. He meditates in other places, but in Thailand he is already enlightened. Perhaps that is why he not only talks but walks. It is also only in Sukothai that he takes these first steps. Perhaps he found them necessary because, as I am discovering, the remains of this old capital are so large. Forty separate compounds cover some forty-three square miles.

I pedal as far as Wat Phra Phai Luang, to the north of the old city walls. This, I am told, may have been the center of the city when it was still land of the Khmers of Angkor. Now it appears suburban with its lake, its sitting Buddha, its pillars and—due to the distance from the entrance—its attractive emptiness, as though it had been abandoned.

Sukothai is certainly not abandoned now. It is one of the most visited of Thai historical sites. And, with the help of UNESCO, the Thai government's art department has done its best to make it attractive. Perhaps, say some, too much.

Indeed, the central section of the ruins are something like a theme park—the thirteenth century seen through contemporary eyes. Nowhere is the result as cosmetic as it is in Sir Arthur Evans's "King Minos' Palace" in Knossos, but the very old wall of the ancient temple breaks down at the precise point where the Buddha inside can be seen to best advantage.

I park my bike, sit on the knoll, look at the reflection of the Buddha of Wat Phra Phai Luang. It is naturally upside-down, and this leads to some reversals in what I have been thinking.

I had been considering the search for the past, the awe with which we regard it. Eyes filled with the dust of history, we do not see what else is there. This is the opposite of the past: not our future (always problematic), but its precise opposite—the present.

I think of New Sukothai, miles down the road, where I am staying, and find it messy, disorganized, inconvenient. And yet, a century from now, some traveler will clasp his or her hands at the thought of someone having really seen the living town of Sukothai.

Me, right here. Is this what the upside-down Buddha, smiling in the depths of the moat, is trying to tell me? Mess, yes, but messiness means vitality. It is neatness, the way the ruins here are tidied up, that speaks of sterility, of death. Thinking, I pedal back through the ancient dust, through the locusts hopping in the heat.

At Mae Hong Son

One of the pleasures of travel is detecting differences. Before we enter a country it is somehow monolithic—all of a piece, like Belgian chocolate or Swiss cheese. Once there, however, whole provinces, whole cantons are found different, even opposite.

I fly from Chiang Mai, a plains city laid out like a garden with its curved avenues, its moated center. The mountains begin in the western suburbs and then stretch further, higher, turning a hazy blue, then deep purple in the distance. Twelve thousand feet below, the slow road, like just-coiled string (it was only completed in 1968) and occasionally disappearing in the crevices of rising mountains.

From the parklike plain the land below thickens into a temperate jungle, great trees, whole orchards of them, all growing at a slant on the increasingly steep mountains. The land crumbles beneath me, small blue lakes appear, streams like arteries. From the flat and placid plain we have come to a vertical and varied land.

Then, below, a few streets, a big stupa, temples, and the prop plane settles on the tarmac. This enormous change has taken under an hour. On the road it would have taken a whole day.

The feeling of being cut off, standing there, watching

further, higher mountains march off to the west, to Burma, the border of which now seems only a mile or two away. This is what all of those exiles, sent here from the capital, must have felt. They called it Siberia.

Yet there is a certain exhilaration in being cut off, standing there confronted by a landscape that's completely different. Or maybe it is just that I know I do not have to stay. Or maybe because Mae Hong Son is now a growing tourist town and its mountain-resort aspects remind me of Switzerland.

With the sudden coolness, all the mountains, all the forests of what look like conifers, the Swiss similarities are reinforced by the architecture — pure Burmese: chalet-style roofs, gingerbread-cut eaves almost reaching the ground, filigreed lacelike roof ridges, what appear to be Gothic-revival doorways. One expects cows and cheese.

Certainly also Swiss-like is the feeling of the benign. Simple seems friendly, placid seems peaceful. And Mae Hong Son is still a small town. Nothing like roaring Bangkok, and even Chiang Mai has traffic lights now. Here in the mountains, I walk along the single shop-lined byway — curry stall, barber shop, travel agent, sundries — and wonder of what it reminds me. Why, Main Street, of course, back when there were Main Streets.

I wonder if it will last. No, of course not. It is not even meant to. Also, it is still Thai, and so it already contains its opposite. This pleasant walk, if trod upon too heavy, will throw up thorns; the silky curry slides gratefully down the throat and only then reveals the pointed needle of the pepper; the Thai roof, a graceful, gentle curve, at the very end suddenly turns and thrusts an upright claw.

Mae Hong Son, says the tourist pamphlet, was founded in 1831 as a camp for the elephants captured in the surrounding jungle. Already dissension—the beasts were for the royal rulers; the difficult and demanding labor of hunting and rearing was made the responsibility of immigrant locals.

These were the Thai Yai, now also known as Shan, presently accounting for half the population of the province, and contributing much to the Burmese look of the place. And now to their numbers have been added thousands of Burmese refugees, driven from their lands by the central government. Tolerated, sometimes assisted, sometimes mistreated by their "hosts," these groups lead a frugal existence in such Burma-border towns as Mae Hong Son.

Those groups in the neighborhood are the Laho, the Misu, the Mon, and the Karen—parts of which are known as Kayan, Karenni, Padaung. They farm, fish, and exhibit themselves. Visiting the "hill tribes" is one of the major tourist attractions of the region.

Among the most popular are the Padaung villages displaying the "long-necked" women. These are individuals who wear brass rings around their necks. Shaped into a continuous coil, they can stand almost a foot in height and weigh almost fifty pounds. This height and heaviness depresses the woman's collarbone, making it appear that the neck is unduly stretched. It must be like wearing a very heavy neck brace, or like being put into a cage, or into some kind of portable stock.

No one agrees on how the custom began. Some say it was to make the women so unattractive that neighboring tribes would abduct them, others that it prevented tigers carrying them off by their throats, others that it was a beauty aid.

Obviously it was the men who made the women wear them, with the same possessive reasoning that in China supported bound feet, in Islamic countries the burqa. One way of coping with such demands is simply to refuse. Women still wear their rings, but the number is declining and their use is no longer mandatory.

Another reason for wearing such a cumbersome and painful contraption, however, is that it makes money. Tourists flock by boat and busload to stare and snap pictures. The villages charge admission, and each "model" usually receives a tip. Such modeling makes more money than farming and fishing combined.

In Mae Hong Son people I talked with assumed that I had come to see the "long-necked" women. I had decided not to. I do not like animal zoos, much less human ones. It is like visiting asylums, prisons, work camps.

But you would be helping them, I was told. Your money gives them food. And they are used to it. Staying away won't help. That was true and, besides, I had a kind of errand there.

A friend in Japan had taken a picture of one of these long-necked women, and he wanted to give it to her, along with a small amount of money. I was to carry both. I had agreed without thinking and now was forced to make up my mind.

I showed the picture to the boatman and expected that he would have no idea where she was. But he recognized her at once. I had no more excuses, her money was in my pocket.

So I got aboard and was paddled downriver to a Karen

village called Nampindin, a muddy little hamlet of straw houses straggling up from the water.

A guide was waiting and not to be ignored. From the age of 5 the women wear their rings, I was told. The first rings weighed more than two pounds. Over the next three or four years, more were piled on. Up until recently there had been twenty-two women living in their neck braces, the oldest being 72. Now there were only eighteen. Women had no sense of civic duty anymore.

Civic duty? Yes. The only reason for continuing the uncomfortable custom was that the money it brought in from the tourists went directly to the Karenni National Progressive Party, an "insurgent" group that wants to establish a separate state in Burma. Though hundreds have fled to Thailand, there were still thought to be some seven helpless and mistreated Karen left over there. Women have their social duty. Please take pictures, pay fees, give tips, and support their cause.

Put that way, reasons for my embarrassment seemed less important. Besides, I reasoned, it was not vulgar curiosity that motivated me but the somehow less specious promise I had made my friend. And I had to hand over the money.

The long-necked lady was found in no time. My unsought guide knew right where she lived. And there she sat, towering, her rings on, long-necked, weaving. Her name was Ms. Matu, and she was 48 years old. She was also something of an icon for the village, decorating as she did many of the postcards for sale.

I gave her the money, which she accepted with quiet dignity, and then showed her my friend's book. She, who had

doubtless seen her picture many, many times before, regarded it patiently. There was a flurry of camera clickings around
us. Other visitors, foreign and Thai alike, were having no
compunctions about photographing. Ms. Matu and the other
women in the compound endured the snapping with dignity
and continued with their weaving.

And I, too, eventually produced a camera and took a
picture of Ms. Matu looking at the picture of herself in my
friend's book. He had certainly suffered no embarrassment
in taking it, and she was having none in regarding it and having her picture again taken doing so. Only I was cringing as I
snapped, and I wondered why.

Well, it was taking advantage of a helpless person, it was
staring at a painful state and doing nothing whatever to alle-
viate it; indeed, it was contributing to its continuations. Ethno-
tourism, that was what it was—and I was handed a receipt
stamped and signed by the "Karenni Culture Department."

I gave Ms. Matu the book in which she appeared, and all
the way back in the boat I wondered about what I had done.

Indeed, one of the pleasures of travel is detecting
differences.

Krabi: The Next Last Paradise

The idea of an unspoiled, untroubled, untouched land
has become necessary in our polluted times—a special space
where nature as it was is still to be discovered and where we
may once more become natural as well. It is a pleasing pros-
pect, this visitable paradise. And one increasingly necessary,

since in our searches we have spoiled earlier paradises. Our very numbers endanger that which we seek. Paradises are polluted when we tourists swarm.

Take Thailand. A country never colonized and thus spared the worst of colonial blight, it still contains pockets of unspoiled shore, untouched sea, places where people and their surroundings seem to exist in that happy symbiosis that is one of the qualifications for a paradise.

The rising tourist tide has, however, taken its toll. Pattaya, a former paradise, is now an Asian Atlantic City. Phuket, which only thirty years ago was still in a state of nature, is now utterly commercialized, its inhabitants quite tourist-weary. The international airport can handle the largest, fullest planes, resorts erupt to house these numbers, development rampages, beach dwindles.

Even the island of Ko Phi-phi, still paradisiacal seen from a distance, now holds highrise hotels, Internet cafés, and "international" cuisine. Leonardo DiCaprio went there, with a film crew that altered the scenery in order to make it seem more paradisiacal.

Not that tourists are solely responsible for the devastation. They are often merely the opportunity for it. It is the Thai who are accountable for inviting in the traveler, making him or her feel at home, and turning a profit. Tourism is a major industry in Thailand, an economically necessary one. Faced with the choice of preserving a paradise and not having enough to eat, I doubt that many of us would hesitate.

In the event, few do. A man I talked to in Phi-phi says that anyone from the governmental environmental protection office attempting to enforce the ban against developing

national park land would probably be driven out by the locals who are making such a killing on the tourists.

And now, I am told, the section of the government responsible for tourist traffic is contemplating a full development of the area south of Phuket, down toward the Malaysian
border, and this includes Trang, Kantang, and Krabi.

Krabi Province contains a number of interesting natural
sites. There is the Ao Luk National Park, which holds Hua
Galok Cave with its 5,000-year-old cave paintings, and the
nearby Lod Cave, through which runs a navigable stream.
The Wat Tham Seua is the most famous of southern forest
temples, but the Phanom Bencha mountain range has barely
been explored. At Klong Thom there are natural hot springs
in the jungle, and the islands of Koh Hong and Koh Phak Bia
hold large tidal chambers surrounded by steep cliffs where
swallow build their valuable nests.

At first glance, the region around Krabi town itself does
not seem too tourist-tempting. Located along a river lined with
mangrove, it has a pleasant riverfront but little else. Once in
the launch, however, and proceeding to the further headland,
the attractions become apparent, and then overwhelming.

This nearest peninsula, the Phra Nang headland, much
resembles Phi-phi. It is a landscape of karst pinnacles, immense limestone towers, the bases scooped by the sea into
fantastic waterways, hidden lakes, flooded caves. Among
these are radiant beaches of white sand, from which one can
look out at standing islands, all soaring straight from the
Andaman Sea, while beneath the waves lies a whole coral
kingdom, with deep caverns and shoals of multicolored fish
swimming in their undersea jungle.

Here is Phra Nang Beach, with its two caverns, its cave-lined walks, its solid walls of climbing stone, and its jungle of virgin coconut trees. In the west is the sunset, and as the declining orb turns the rocks russet, then gold, one sees again the beauty our world once held.

Here then is a paradise, even an Eden. Overhead, forest birds soar, while below gibbons swing through the trees. Large but harmless monitor lizards stalk the paths, and hundreds of butterflies swirl in the morning air. One thinks of the ancient Islands of the Blessed—or of Maxfield Parrish, or Steven Spielberg, or James Bond, according to one's tastes.

Just offshore stand two karst islands, dubbed the Happy Isles and looking like something in a Sung painting. At low tide one may slosh through tamed waves to the tiny hidden beaches or take canoes to paddle through the sea caves. Or you may make the steep climb up and into the Tham Phranang to reach a large salt-water lagoon, the Sra Phranang, which surges twice a day. And, all day long, at the Pan Mao Beach, the sunrise beach to the east, there is rock climbing for both initiate and amateur.

Historically, the place is more Bond than not. It was an area of ancient violence, much favored by pirates who hid in the coves and ventured forth to attack passing ships. One such held a beautiful Indian princess, a typhoon sank the imperial vessel, pirates swarmed, and in the great Tham Phranang Cave now stand two spirit houses dedicated to the unfortunate royal and giving the beach its name.

For how long can such a place continue, I wonder. One authority on the area has written that latter-day pirates now steal islands or parts of islands for development. Sooner or later all of this nature will disappear, but at present the Phra Nang area has a better chance of survival than others. It is surrounded by national park land, and the Thai Queen Mother has her summer palace nearby—a favorite view includes just this stretch of landscape.

In addition, the major place to stay on the peninsula, the Rayavadee Premier Resort, is so eco-friendly that it has already won a number of awards, one of them the 1998 Office of Environmental Policy and Planning Best Hotel Award for Reducing Environmental Damage.

The headland can be reached only by boat, because it is set off by these enormous karst barriers and deep swaths of jungle. Everything, including all the food and amenities, must come by boat, usually from Phuket, and the tourist must also make interesting but inconvenient trips from Krabi by vehicle, transferring to a launch. All of this helps brake mass tourism.

This and the price. Though there are a few backpack-friendly areas on the headland, even these cannot be as cheap as those elsewhere. The rock climbers have to walk a distance, pay a bit, and their accommodations are subdued. No beach buggies, no power skis. There are beer halls and prole grub places, but there are also a lot of signs that read: Please Be Quiet.

If one stays at the pristine Rayavadee, one pays a price that is unusually high for Thailand, but in return one gets a contemporary paradise. It is worth it, since the bill keeps big tour groups out. If, on the other hand, you like your paradises populated, there are other places up the coast, and then there is always Pattaya.

Paradise—that place where somebody finds perfect

happiness. But first one must consider what perfect happiness consists of. I lie on the warm sand and feel the hot sun seep into me, warming my cold core.

The lisp of the shallow waves murmurs in my ears, and when I raise my eyes they are full of the blue sea and the distant piles of hills and forest, fabled isles of the blessed. Then perhaps also a helping hand, dexterous and oiled, the beach massage. Am I happy?

On January 15, 1850, Flaubert wrote to Louis Bouilhet about his traveling companion, the writer and photographer Maxime Du Camp: "Max had himself jacked off the other day in a deserted section among some ruins and said it was very good." What a fine image of the romantic Orientalist taking advantage of his position—as passing tourist, as someone with more money.

Why are tourists so horny? Well, they are someplace where they are unknown, so no prying eyes and prattling tongues. And they have time, something concupiscence takes lots of. But, perhaps most important, sex means sense of self. Alone in a new environment, cut from the past and plunked into an alien present, they are grasping for the straws of identity. Sex is gratifying. Not only is it pleasurable, it is also a sign that one still has a bit of power, that one is still someone: oneself.

Maybe that is why the delightful distractions of travel are so often accompanied by the known certainties of lust. One balances the other. And there is also the paradisiacal condition. Harps and haloes are not sufficient for today's visitable paradise. It is, after all, a place, situation, or condition in which somebody finds perfect satisfaction.

BURMA

Country at the Crossroads

Rangoon (or Yangon as it is now called) seen from the air seems subdued, at least after brilliant nighttime Bangkok. Just a light here and there, otherwise a carpet of darkness. This extends even down into the new and otherwise imposing airport where the light is so dim that officials squint to read my visa.

After the ordinary airport glare of just about everywhere else this obscurity seems attractively somber, and I remark upon and am told that the effect is not deliberate, that it was due to frequent electric power grid breakdowns and the fear that more will occur if the light level is turned up.

This was my introduction to one of the many structural breakdowns occurring in unhappy Burma, caught in the grip of a restrictive regime for decades now, the bureaucracy of the military junta having held the country since 1962.

But the illusion that dimness is more natural than brightness continued, and I found the city so shadowy, so full of groves, stands of trees, and clutches of bushes, that I was reminded of a much less scrubbed Singapore or of a more decaying Savanna. This illusion I ascribed to the pull of the past, an old-fashioned quality, a kind of temporal poverty toward which I am drawn.

There is a palpable past of Asia itself, the beauty of things that lives on long after their usefulness has evaporated. In Rangoon, this is embellished with the more recent colonial past. We pass the Strand Hotel, now refurbished, repainted, restored, though not yet gentrified in the manner of Singapore's Raffles. It speaks not of English power but of English gentility, smiling away on the dark street and suggesting that by comparison we weren't so bad after all, were we?

But I'm not going to stay there. A bed there, despite the country's poverty, costs almost as much as one in Tokyo's Ritz-Carlton or at the Hong Kong Peninsula. Nor am I going to stay at any of the government-owned hotels. (Though in a sense the government already owns everything; it gets about a third of your bill no matter where you stay.) You can tell the government hotels at a glance: they are often named after the city or the local sight, and they have the national flag flying in front, something private hotels only occasionally do; also, the best guides (i.e., *Lonely Planet*) refuse to list them.

Why do I have this aversion? Because I am prejudiced. What I have heard about the government here almost convinced me not to come at all, and once here it finds me unwilling to call the place Myanmar, a name the government began insisting upon in 1989. I have never been to any country under such circumstances—distrusting the governance of the place. In the rain, aware of a pervading melancholy, I proceed to my modest hotel.

❊

In the morning the sky clears, the sun appears, and what I see resembles what the English must have seen a century ago. There are few cars and trucks and bikes, and many people still wearing Burmese clothes—skirt-like *longyi* for the men. There is a thriving market-culture. Goods for sale on the streets, piles of mango and papaya. People carry bundles on their heads. I see an ox-cart or two.

And the colors, all pastel shades after the loud primaries of Thailand: rose, beige, a soft verdigris, and a strange and ubiquitous yellow. It is pale, near white, and I see it not only on temple walls but also on the cheeks and foreheads of men and women on the street. Like clay it is applied in squares or circles to the face, and though I am told it forms some kind of sunscreen, it in actuality is a fashion. Almost no one young is without it, sometimes accented by the scarlet lips and crimson tongue of the betel chewer. The stuff is called *thanakha* and is derived from the bark of a tree. It has a smell—and probably a taste as well.

My street scene, once I am a part of it, is redolent with scent—ripening fruit, sweat, incense, dung. I take a taxi on this hot morning, and the driver has hung a flowering branch of jasmine in front of the air conditioner so that its fragrance will flavor my journey.

❋

Avoiding the state-owned Myanma Airways, I take one of the semiprivate lines (there are several: Air Bagan, Air Mandalay, Yangon Airways) to the ancient ecclesiastic city of Pagan (Bagan). It is on an enormous plain along the

Ayeyarwady River. About sixteen miles square, it holds some 2,237 temples, most of them ancient and enormous relics of the great capital that existed here from around A.D. 1047 and that was abandoned at the approach of Kublai Khan's raiders in 1287.

It is an astonishing place, stupas as far as you can see, as though you were a tiny pawn in a mighty chess game, the pieces of which tower in all directions. It is like being at Angkor Wat with all the jungle cleared away, the distance palpable. It is like all the churches in Europe crushed into a single shire. And, with their red-brick crenellated walls, their turrets and stone fretwork, the buildings, despite their age, look somehow Victorian, as though thousands of stately homes had been scattered on the plain, an effect enhanced by the many winding country roads and the horse carts trotting along them. The scene is somehow late nineteenth century, and there seems something ostentatious in the ornate wedding-cake architectural styles, in the deserted sumptuousness of this whole, vast, empty ecclesiastical city — all temples and stupas — that lies there like an abandoned Vatican.

*

Here any place the tourists come the children gather. They are garlanded with postcards, loaded with handicrafts, burdened with books. Many carry around smudged stacks of a pirated edition of Penguin's *Burmese Days* by George Orwell — all for sale as these small salespeople try to pry some dollars loose. I had never before, even in Cambodia, seen such a shameless display of forced child labor and wondered what the socialist Orwell would have made of such an extreme example of capitalism. And I tried to imagine a poverty that made necessary the sending of such small children out to vend things.

One little girl, five or so, attached herself to me. Wherever I went she was there too, calling out in a small and gentle voice, deaf to my repeated no-thanks, following like a shadow or a bad conscience, The children have apparently been taught by whoever controls them to allocate their prospects. Even as a covey of tourists approaches, each child is sizing up the group, selecting the most likely. She had seen some promise in me.

Even after I had bought my string of Pagan postcards, even after I had climbed back into my pony cart, there she stood, perhaps hoping I would buy more, perhaps thinking of the next encounter, perhaps not thinking at all. As we trotted off I waved, a facetious yet friendly gesture, but she did not wave back.

❖

Contemplating the ancient capital, I asked about the new one, Naypyidaw. Carved out of the jungle, it was built, like Brasilia, to house the government, and at an enormous expense (estimated at $300 million) in one of the world's poorest countries. "Oh, that," I was told by a young woman at the hotel, "We call it the New Cemetery."

When I asked why she said it was because of the age of the inhabitants. The senior general of the controlling junta is now nearly 80 years old and his peers are not much younger.

They will not be around much longer. It is as though they built this brand new concrete stupa collection in order to have a place to die in.

I had seen other signs of candor as well. In my room was a notice: "Dear Guests: Due to poor postage systems, your postcard may take some time to reach, or even may not always reach to your address." Later I was told a joke. I asked about television and was told: "We have two TV channels—one for the military, and one for the soldiers."

Soldiers are not popular. I see very few and these only from a distance. They are apparently brought out promptly enough when there is work for them to do, such as subduing people protesting the government. I am told, however, that the job is now more often handed over to gangs of the otherwise unemployed, those so poor that they will beat up their neighbors.

Unpopular though soldiers are in Burma, the profession offers a way out for those whom poverty has otherwise blocked. If you join the army you are taken care of; everything is free. If you keep your nose clean some advancement seems possible. This is often perceived as a better life than selling postcards to tourists. The consequence is a 375,000-member army, one that has nearly doubled in size over the past decade.

❉

Another option is becoming a monk. Here you are taken care of, though with nothing like the generosity the army extends. You must beg, as is the Buddhist tradition, and besides the maroon robe among the few belongings a monk is allowed is his begging bowl. Becoming a monk is still regarded as an honor, something that becoming a soldier does not seem to be.

In Mandalay I had lunch with well over a thousand monks at the Maha Ganayon Kyaung temple complex. It was they who ate, however. I merely watched. Around eleven in the morning they gather in long lines, young men, adolescents, children, all in deep red habits, all with shaved heads, holding their bowls before them. In the courtyard huge vats of cooked rice are steaming, attended by whoever has volunteered to do the serving—people from the neighborhood, temple persons, I saw two tourists at work as well and wished that I had volunteered.

To witness a ceremony like this is to want to be a part of it. It was so orderly. More than a thousand people (1,400 that day I was later told), men and boys, waited in complete silence. The lines were long but their attitude was exemplary. There was no anticipation (though they are allowed only two meals a day, an early breakfast and this midday meal, nothing at all in the evening), no impatience.

Eating was obviously a serious ritual. These thousands of pairs of eyes looked straight ahead. Tourist cameras clicked but there were no smiles. Remembering the cheerful monks of Thailand (same religion, Theravada Buddhism), I found the sobriety impressive. It felt as though these thousands who had merely assembled to be fed had other things in mind. Slowly, orderly, the lines moved forward as though inexorable.

✻

An unemployed guide, a middle-age man, balding but not yet married, still saving his money, he said, told me about wages in Burma. A lower-class worker makes about 500 kyat ($1.20) a day; government teachers make $21 a month—an amount even less. Many people have to live on less than $1 a day. Girls, however, could get from $25 to $125 a night if they were lucky. He'd take me to the discotheques in Rangoon if I didn't believe him and show me himself.

The problem, one of the problems, he told me was that there is no free education. Every level, from primary school through university, costs money. A result is that the people of this country—in 1945 considered one of the most economically promising—are now among the poorest in Asia. Over decades of bad governance, ever since the military junta seized power in 1962, education in particular has been neglected. His generation, he said, might be the last that could produce doctors, teachers. His children would not know enough to.

Living with the junta's dictatorship has left people frightened. There are 53 million people in the country, he told me, and most them are afraid. They have learned to always be looking around for signs of danger, neighbors spy on neighbors, and there is no freedom of movement. Under "internal security laws" people have to register with so-called immigration officials if they travel even from one town to another.

At that point our car was stopped by several young men who stepped out from the side of the road. One of them held his hand out, then just as quickly drew it back and we drove on. "He saw you," I was told.

I asked if these were robbers. Not really, he said. Each neighborhood had to fix its own roads since no governmental offices did, so those that used the roads had to contribute, and the only way to get them to do so was to bar their progress until they did so. Then he said the part about their backing off at seeing a foreigner in the back seat was a joke. I told him not to worry, that I was not going to report any of this.

"No," he told me, "you go on and talk about it, write about it. Me, I don't care. I been arrested, I been in jail, and so I decided not to be scared anymore. If everyone stopped being afraid then maybe something would happen."

Lots to be afraid of. Millions of people falling into poverty in a country with a per capita gross domestic product that is behind even Uganda's, and a government guilty of gross mismanagement, of ignorance, of cronyism, of hostility to all advice—now a bloated, cancerous bureaucracy, retrenched and lashing out at suspected reformers.

And in its own way just as desperate as the people it tyrannizes. Hence the fivefold increase in the price of gas, the doubling of diesel prices, the collapse of the bus system. There's over fifty percent inflation, I was told. They have to cut costs.

But the road is lined with piles of canisters, with big plastic screw-top containers, with buckets. The vendors call out as we pass. When I ask what they are selling I am told that it is gasoline. Black-market fuel, to be sold at enormously inflated prices to desperate motorists whose cars have stopped. Since the government sells most of the gas and oil abroad, to China at present, in order to get cash, the people down the line resort to this—gouging each other.

❊

From the wharf at Mandalay I take a small boat upriver to ancient Mingun, one of the old royal capitals. The trip is enchanting. We putt along a shore where women are doing their wash in the river, beating the cloth against the stones, where the children run naked, somersaulting into the ocher water, where men higher up on the bank are working with their buffalos, or fishing, or just sitting. It is like a living frieze, the very picture of how people live naturally, a snapshot from the Golden Age.

Except that it isn't to anyone except me. It certainly isn't to the women kneeling while beating the rocks with their laundry. The guide tells me that only a quarter of the population still farms and that this is becoming more and more difficult. How about the rest? They are mostly government employees now, he says. He adds that Mandalay is now about half Chinese, though Rangoon is still only about five percent. I look at all the natural beauty, the unspoiled bank, the lithe and beautiful children, and remember that everyone is somehow living on a dollar a day.

Up ahead Mingun looms—a stand of trees, a white temple stupa, the Settawya Paya where a footprint of the Buddha is enshrined, and dwarfing everything else the mighty base of the Mingun Paya. This enormous structure was to provide the foundation for the highest stupa in the world. Nearly five hundred feet it was to tower, high enough that King Bodawpaya could look over the nearby mountain and see if the enemy was coming. This was in 1790.

Thousands of slaves and prisoners-of-war were to labor

there, and the king himself supervised the work, from an off-shore palace he had especially constructed, until he died in 1819, when the whole enormous folly was abandoned. Nature then decided to help; an 1838 earthquake split the unfinished monument and reduced it to the impressive square of rubble it is at present. And there it stands, a monument to futility, its façade riven by the earthquake, a long vertical fissure like a slash in the face.

As though to savor the contrast, we went across the road to the Buddhist Infirmary, a kind of hospice, a nursing home for the elderly, run by the monks and the nuns. A group of low, white-washed buildings holds long dormitories, a ward with many beds. In each, or on the porch, or sitting in the sun, were the old men (old women have a separate building), who nodded and smiled and would willingly have talked if I spoke Burmese. I would have asked about what they had seen, about the changes in their long lives, about what they remembered. But as it was I merely left some money and received some smiles and a blessing, and then boated back.

What remains of the royal endeavor is a tourist destination, the terminus of a boat trip, a scratch on the face of time. But remain it does. That evening as the sun was going down, casting its long rays up the river, I looked from my hotel window and saw, ten miles across the valley, on the opposite shores of the distant mud-colored river, a tiny white square, turning pink, invisible unless you knew where to look, the Mingun Paya, and somewhere beneath it, hidden in the shadow, the Buddhist Infirmary.

❋

Burma made me think. I had seen the living past, framed my scenes from the Golden Age, glimpsed a kind of symbiotic order not now often encountered—and I had seen the bill: what this cost in modern terms, in misery and in hopelessness. The very qualities that constituted my view of the past were now penalties that the modern world imposed. Arcady now meant poverty.

Here in Burma this became visible because the cause was visible. Not merely the laws of economics but a power that was bending them as it desired, not merely something unfortunate that was somehow also natural but a dark authority bent only upon its own continuation.

In Burma I had a contrast, a duality. I could define what I was searching for through the lineaments of its opposite. In the beauty, the charm, the innocence of people I met, I could see their opposite—stern, implacable.

That evening, my last in the country—I was becoming increasingly claustrophobic—I was taken to the marionette theater, the *youq-the pwe*, a whole world in miniature. There are forty-eight puppets—the god, the royal family, the regent, the pages, an old man and an old woman and a hermit. There is one villain but four ministers and two clowns—one good, one bad. In addition there is a horse, a monkey, a serpent, and an elephant. These characters are enacted by dolls three or so feet high, hung on as many as sixty strings including one each for each eyebrow.

These people dash from one side of the proscenium to the other and treat each other quite roughly. Royal though they are, they are forever slapping each other, the animals are always chasing them, and the clowns are always getting in their way. There is a Punch and Judy look to their antics, but the puppets predate the British. They indicate an earlier age, the period of the Mandalay kingdoms of the eighteenth century when royalty had all of the privileges and most of the responsibilities.

The skill with which these dolls are moved about is extraordinary. Clowns dance, maidens pine, animals are ridden on and off. There are real sword fights and there is real lovemaking. We almost, as in the Japanese Bunraku, believe in them. Then, suddenly, the curtain is further raised, and we see a backstage full of grown men manipulating these now child-sized dolls, pulling their strings, deftly switching the controls from right to left, while the puppets leap and pirouette, or stop and sigh, or collapse in a weeping heap on the floor.

Watching the puppets, one of the last things I did in Burma, seemed salutary. Not so much beneficial as fitting, as though I had seen an allegory. Those men in control were only men. They would be replaced. They had simply become their job. They themselves were more puppets than the puppets they animated. The puppets are more real; they had survived from long before.

BORNEO

The Long Houses of the Iban

From Kuching it is an hour by car and another hour by boat to Bako, a peninsula where the jungle is black as basalt, where monitor lizards slide over the rocks and the mangroves show their great brown knees in the lowering tide where our beached boat now lies.

We—me and a guide named Abu—slipped into the still and steamy forest, and at once there was silence—no bird calls, no animal scurryings. We followed a trail over vine-gripped rocks, through puddles of mud thick as soup; climbed over the ridges, down into black-green valleys where mosquitoes whined. I was soon winded, but the weight of the jungle prevented my paying much attention—it was too fascinating to be thinking about myself.

Abu put out a hand and kept me from colliding with a thorn tree as large around as I was, then pointed to a moving rope at my feet. Black ants, very tenacious when disturbed. Then the trees uncoiled and grass appeared—a small glade lay ahead, and Abu put his finger to his lips. We heard the sound, a purposeful thrashing in the branches ahead. Softly, silently, he led me through the patches of sunlight toward the noise and then pointed.

Ahead, amid the branches, there appeared a near-human

head, one as large as mine. The small brown eyes stared, between them a long and bulb-shaped nose. Then it seemed to have seen us, and with a turn it was gone, its thrashings dying as it fled over the ridge. It was a proboscis monkey—and this forest is one of their few homes.

Back in Kuching I picked off the leeches, shook out the ants, and took a hot shower—then in the cool of the early evening walked the sinuous riverfront, recently constructed, full of trees and benches and wharves, maybe like Bangkok a hundred years ago—still faintly redolent of the colonial, a lavender-like scent, now mixed with the earth odor of Borneo and its smells of coriander and chili. Though high-rises are going up, and two international-chain hotels have opened, though some USA junk-food outlets gape on the banks, the muddy charms of Borneo are also there, wide eyes, smiles, a natural quiet, a pace still slow.

✻

In the morning a car picks me up and we begin the four-hour drive inland. The road gently climbs until finally the great mountains of Kalimantan (the Indonesian half of this enormous island) are standing blue in the distance. It then turns and climbs over the ridges and shortly goes off onto a bumpy dirt road that gets more and more narrow, and finally stops at the edge of an enormous lake. We are at Batang Ai, the origin of a great river that flows back to the South China Sea.

A boat is waiting. The driver promises to return in a few days, and I set off over the still lake, flat and silver in the cloudy late afternoon. On the far shore, just a line, I can make out long, low buildings—these are long houses, I thought, home of head-hunters. And so they were, though of a special kind, as I discovered when the boat docked and we climbed up into the lobby and checked into the Hilton Batang Ai Longhouse Resort.

It is an enormous place, with room for more than a hundred guests, facilities for all meals, generators for the electricity, water purification plant, swimming pool, and a full staff. The water comes from the lake, and most of the food is local. Since Sarawak is protecting this entire swath of jungle, the resort is not allowed to fell any trees, the sewage is treated, there is a national grid and so no oil or smoke, garbage is carted back, and supplies are carted in. In addition, most of the staff is local. There is even a resident naturalist on hand, with his own office right off the lobby.

My room is high-ceilinged, a replica of a large long house chamber, but with air conditioning, running water, toilet, and much else that an Iban long house does not have. It is to their country that I have come, and I now find myself in a luxurious and expensive replica.

We late travelers always carry with us our shell. We are like the hermit crab that cannot move unless he surrounds himself with his chosen environment. I saw one once taken from the handsome shell he had appropriated. There was, it turned out, nothing to him, just a head with a neck and front claws. Otherwise, a body more like a tail, now curling spasmodically as though to pull himself into a shelter no longer there. He was put on the table and could not even walk—he had traveled by pulling his shell along as though it were some kind of vehicle.

I had traveled in the carapace of the car, the shell of the boat, and was now in the copious container of the Hilton's fake long house. Though I ate well, a local catfish *meuniere*, and soundly slept to the lisping of the lake, I also determined that in the morning I would crawl from my shell and see the real world.

✻

So the next day I made arrangements for a guide, a local named James, to take me to Spaya on the Engkari River. This is two hours by long boat and is the nearest sizeable Iban long house settlement.

I had to sit very still—long boats easily and often tip over—but soon lost any concern as the river began to turn, disclosing new and further vistas, and the beauty of the Borneo jungle closed in. The water was as clear as the lake, and in the depths below us swam large fish—perhaps the kind I had eaten at supper the night before—fat as bass but with a pointed head like a pike. The sun shone hot and the great silent jungle slid past, and finally we made another turn and there was Spaya.

The long houses were real ones, built steep on stilts, tall up on the banks where the highest of waters would not reach. Perhaps once thatched, they now sported roofs of zinc, yet were still held together by untidy ropes that had been made by hand. We walked up to them and then climbed the ladders.

There seemed no one there until we had climbed into the first house, but we heard voices in the dark and soon saw, in the next room, stretched along the length of the bamboo floor, women and children. They looked up and smiled, not at all surprised to see us. Of course they had heard the long boat motor and had followed the silence of the jungle as it quieted at our approach. The men, James explained, were at work in the fields, for these Iban are farmers.

We were invited to sit down and given rice wine, then left alone. *What was going to happen?* I asked James. *Everything happens in its own time*, was his reasoned reply, and a small child came and sat beside me to stare as I watched the communal life going on around me.

At first everything seemed squalid. The interior was a mess, with pigs grunting far below, under the floor, and people aimlessly picking things up and putting things down. But I had not been there half an hour before I began to detect order. Things are stored together by shape (because they take less room that way) and also by analogy—things to be used (feathers, thread, string) were kept distinct from things already used (cloth, bark).

Work was also allocated—all that picking things up and putting things down. Near me, a young girl had been splitting wood, then she put down the hatchet and went away. An old woman came up and started splitting the wood, and after her a large child. Then the young girl came back and continued just as though she had never stopped. There was no telling anyone to do anything, and no discussion of the work at all. No one seemed in charge.

I had come across what looked like a perfect democracy.

It probably isn't. Maybe when the men come back in the evening there is some show of authority, but I don't think so; the cooperation seemed too practiced.

I watched this patterned life and began to understand how basic—that is, how human it was. Despite the Gatorade T-shirt on one of the girls, Adidas running pants on one of the boys, I was looking at something eternal, something that had always been—like the jungle. Yet now it was so rare that these people seemed to me . . . well, innocent.

Now why would I think that? Perhaps because travel is more than a transversal of space. It is also displacement in time. I am here peering as though through a telescope held wrong way round, at a time seemingly much earlier than my own. Just as we sometimes see children as innocent simply because we are older, I look at the Iban and detect something childlike. And from the back of my head steal forth related notions: fatal knowledge, blessed ignorance, original sin, and the like. So I choose innocence and feel the moist pleasure that comes with this.

How to live where space reticulates, where sounds have shades, where feelings weigh something? I no longer live this way, have long forgotten how, and then I see hanging on the walls, from the rafters, what I identify as fetishes: bits of string and twig, a bamboo triangle, a mannikin made of mud. All of these look down at me and I know that we are innocent if we feel constantly under the regard of a god, if we feel that he is always there, like a father.

In unspoken agreement the wives and children sat down, an old woman brought out a large drum, another dragged in a full set of gongs, and we were entertained. An old man put on a feathered headdress and did a slow, turning dance—one that showed his tattoos, geometric indigo designed against his tan skin. Then a girl, just out of childhood, smiled and to the beat of the drum danced, her feet together, her arms and hands alive with movement. Then a young man danced. He had a wooden sword and his poses turned into stompings and leaps as something—a hunt, a kill—was mimed, until he became confused or embarrassed, rubbed his head, and stopped.

But the drums and gongs continued. We sat there thinking it a concert until James told me that it was our turn—Iban hospitality insisted upon it. He imitated the hunting leaps and feints very well, and I shuffled about doing what I remembered of the hand gestures.

Then we were taken to the guest room—a part of the long house—and told to eat the lunches that James had brought from the resort. Two girls and three young men sat opposite us and stared, as did the old man with tattoos and the old woman who had played the drum.

We were naturally unable to eat, because they were not eating and though James had told me that they usually ate when they wanted and had no lunch hours, nonetheless I gave one of my sandwiches to the old woman and the other to the tattooed old man. The fruit we'd brought I gave to them all, and the woman put it on the table and then meticulously cut everything up, making perfect piles, one for each one of them.

James said that this was the way it always was, and that was why our bags, all untended, were perfectly safe. Once we were in the community, no one stole and no one cheated.

The old man ate his tangerine slice and told me (with James's help) that he was 85. The girl said she was still 12.

Munching, I looked at the ceiling and saw four or five large baskets of skulls, the contents of all of them looking at me. I then remembered that the people of native Borneo were sometime head-hunters. James, misunderstanding my sudden interest, told me that I was a temporary member and could take pictures of them if I wished. But I did not want to and asked him if they still took heads. He laughed and said, no, not at all. I asked when the last head was taken and he said 1992 — but that it was kind of an accident.

After dinner some of the boys and girls brought out what they had made — obviously for sale, but they did not know how much anything should cost. From the boy in the blue Adidas I bought a carving of a monkey in a tree and finally managed to make them take what I thought it was worth, which it turned out was double what they had decided to ask.

In so doing I was spoiling the fun of later tourists, all set to haggle; but there were no tourists yet (except me), though there certainly will be. The trusting Iban with their lack of business expertise — what will they be like in a year from now, what with the Hilton right next door?

In thanks, as it were, the old man came and indicated that I might feel his tattoos. Then the young men offered arms and legs and the girls gave me their hands to examine. In turn I was then pawed over, but James, perhaps Iban himself, was left alone.

Our visit done, we were accompanied back to the boat and from the water saw the boys and girls solemnly lined up.

No electricity, no radio, no TV, these people were (for the time being) living life as it once was—everyone's life as it had been. In going upriver through the jungle I had come to my own childhood, and I wanted to stay, to be a part of something this natural, this wholesome.

But I wasn't, couldn't, and didn't. Perhaps I had glimpsed my own childhood, but I was no longer a child, and before we had gone round the first bend this innocent and practical people had gone back to their late afternoon lives, into which our coming had created the merest ripple.

KOREA

A Divided Land

The world from above, from the window of the plane — I
look down and there lie the patterns, a mold of the country,
the shape of its habits. England, a patchwork quilt, all private
parishes and parks; America, great rectangles, all that space,
that openness, as though everyone owns everything; Japan,
the tidy geometrics demanded by rice, the curves that satisfy
tea; over Korea, land broken by mountains, something northern, one expects snow, even in summer, an Asian Norway, at
the same time a rug of contrasting shapes, no two the same, a
landscape that seems to speak of argument and compromise.
Or does it? Or am I merely casting thoughts down onto the
blameless earth beneath me?

In a small plane, Seoul to Sorak, I fly to the eastern coast,
up and along the misty grays and tans of middle Korea and
then over the mountains, seen flat from above, long afternoon
shadows showing their real height, then beneath me again
the sudden green of a valley, a cold river, bright and brown.

Very difficult to capture, in paint, in words, this instant
green, this precise brown, like something just made, just
born. Yet, the colors are familiar — Cézanne colors. He found
them half a world away; I find them here.

That painter once said: Paint what you see, not what you

know is there. Good advice—for how often do I catch myself casting my shadow on what I see and finding a meaning in what I already believe.

⁂

The landscape of Korea seems freely apportioned, freshly painted, but the view from the air cannot show the defining fissure, the division that rends the land. The Korean Peninsula is divided in half. The bottom half is the Republic of Korea, South Korea, the smaller (small, same size as America's Virginia); the larger rest is the Democratic People's Republic of Korea, North Korea.

The two are separated at the 38th parallel by the DMZ (Demilitarized Zone) that cuts across the peninsula from sea to sea. It was created by a kind of international agreement, but the conflict has never found a political or a diplomatic solution and South Korea has never been a signatory. There is still a civil war going on, North against South, reminders everywhere.

The two-hour bus ride down the coast to Kangnung. Beautiful beaches but all fenced off. All military land. The North is near. Plane passengers taking off from here, or landing, must lower their window shades so that they do not see the forbidden view.

Of what does this forbidden view consist? Passengers are never told, never ask. To be a Korean is to live in a divided land. No matter how clean, how crisp, how fresh, the place also contains the echoes from another Korea, just to the north.

I remember divided Berlin where East and West (rather than North and South) were the appointed directions of poverty and plenty. One half of the country defining itself through the other half—by comparison with East Berlin the West found itself free, democratic; by comparison with West Berlin, the East found itself poor but also somehow politically, puritanically, more pure.

Korea is like this. The South feels sorry for the deprived North and would like to incorporate it. The North, shivering, sees the South as politically compromised. Yet how they feel about themselves is completely conditioned by the proximity of a neighbor presumed opposite.

The South wants a unified land. At the same time it fears the enormous exodus that would occur once the dividing line is rubbed out, once the gates are open, once the starving North falls on the fertile South.

*

In Kangnung, the riverbed, the great yearly Tano Festival: tents, parades, fireworks, the farmers' dance, poetry contests, games, a circus—small children flying through the air, a father balancing his babe on his feet, a magician pulling the entire Korean national flag out of his mouth; Korean wrestling (young boys in red robes straining and pulling, falling with great thumps onto the sand); potato pancakes with chives, whole pig heads, great gutted fish, candied apples, sticky syrups, barrels of the potent *soju*.

Each tent is a cornucopia, overflowing with food and drink, the very picture of fertility. I am reminded of Flemish paintings of whole landscapes of the edible, of Brueghel's pictures of peasant feasts. Grilled pork, marinated; beef ribs with turnips, mushrooms, and nuts; sausages with onion stuffing; grilled beef strips with soy sauce, sesame oil, pepper, garlic and sugar; octopus stew, seafood boiled in bean-paste; broiled mackerel; steamed snapper; abalone porridge; fish-cake soup in beef stock; codfish soup; steamed clams; noodles with meat, vegetables, eggs and red pepper paste. And, everywhere, *kimch'i* — seasoned, fermented cabbage or turnip or radish or cucumber, marinated in crushed red pepper, garlic, salt — along with lots else (apples, pears, anchovies), all eaten fresh or ripe or sour, and coming in two hundred different varieties. And somewhere in this mass of tents, these avenues of appetite, smaller venues for unapproved delicacies where, if I searched, I could find grilled snake, earthworm soup, boiled dog.

The variety is astonishing — and everything is so fresh. Korean food is so firm, so crisp, so somehow new. It is food as though tasted for the first time. It is like the mountain water — good, sweet water, so cold the teeth ache, and one's thirst is forever as the water pours down the throat like down the mountain itself. Like the people too — direct, straight looks, everything really what it looks like, everything new. What is this renewal? Here I see, hear, smell, taste, think, feel more than ever before. It is perhaps that here I live right now, right in the present.

To live in the present. No memory, no expectation. What joy. Is this how we are meant to live? Each repeated experience always new. Known yesterday, a novelty today. No conception of tomorrow. Instead a world full of sights and sounds and smells and tastes, every second new. Is it travel alone that creates this feeling of promise? Where we live, home, we inhabit only an eternal and unsatisfying future. Here in Korea the flesh is firm and immediate and the food is just caught, and the thought is just invented.

⁂

Elsewhere in this vast field by a stream leading to the sea, another city of tents where amid shouts, screams, waving fans, and paper streamers shamans incantate, looking through closed eyes into the past.

Shamanism is Korea's earliest religious belief and one that still maintains. It is pantheistic and animist, and it attributes spirits to all things. There are a vast number of these, nearly three hundred categories of deities making up, including the subcategories, some 10,000 spirits. This has been determined both by the shamans and by those university professors who study them.

The vast numbers of spirits need equally large numbers of shamans. There are some 300,000 registered in South Korea, which means one shaman for every 160 South Koreans. They are all independent, each following different deities, sharing no body of scripture, and all are markedly adaptable. During the pro-American days a familiar spirit was that of General Douglas MacArthur, and when his spirit took possession the shaman put on sunglasses, sucked on a pipe, and made noises that some mistook for English. Nowadays shamans have been among the earliest to use commercial

Web sites, offering online fortune-tellin
pages.

A shaman specialty is communicatin
eryone has a loved one or two in the gre
they would like to hear from. Shamans
medium for the astral flow, the spiritu
necessary for the communication.

There are formulas for obtaining this. The shaman ritual
is in three sections: there is an evocation of the spirits, then
some entertainment for them once they have appeared, and
finally their being sent off. Based on this formula are the four
ceremonies: one for the rest of the dead, one for the healing
of the living, one for good fortune, and one for initiations of
new shamans.

The spirits themselves are no problem. Shamans believe
they are just everywhere; the air is thick with them, everywhere crowded with the dead all anxious to have a word or
two.

Another specialty is not only populating the past but also
envisioning the future, indeed, experiencing it. A shaman
consulted by someone with stomach pains will go through
cancer itself, if that is what it is. Pregnancies induce something like it in the medium—a possibility since almost all Korean shamans are *mudang*, that is, female, all the *paksu* (male)
having been demonized away by the prevailing Christians
and the government. The future lies an open book before the
all-seeing eye of the shaman, and the telling of coming for-
tunes is plain, there on the opened page.

All of these various beliefs have resulted in an extraordinary religious eclecticism that has much influenced Korea's

toward belief and made it one of the most religiously
alistic of countries—somewhere where Confucianism,
Buddhism, and Christianity peacefully coexist and indeed
overlap. Korean religions, particularly shamanism, is seen as
materialistic, very concerned with this world of ours, and
this is something it might be said most Koreans also tend to
be.

With the help of an English-speaking Korean student
hoping that the results would unlock the further mysteries of
that language, I am sat in front of a large woman in a brightly
striped garment, stone necklaces around her neck, turquoise
earrings, gold teeth, who says that she will be summoning one
of my forefathers. No, she does not yet know which one—he
has to come a long way and she cannot yet identify him, so
small is he in the distance of time.

Closing her eyes, holding one hand over my head, the
shaman begins in a low voice to hum, the pitch rising, apparently, with the approach of the distant spirit. The closer he
gets, this forefather of mine, the higher and the louder grows
the chanting that the hum has become. Sweat appears on that
broad face in front of me and the gold teeth flash. Then with
a bound this big woman is standing, dancing as though strug-
gling with some unseen opponent, and the stone necklaces
tinkle and the keening grows higher still.

Then she is suddenly still, and the possessing spirit
stands before me. He looks just like her but he acts differ-
ently. He leans down, wants to pat my head, shake my hand,
a forefather meeting his future ancestor. Also he speaks
what my student helper seriously informed me was English.
Later, when I ask what it was that my dead forefather said,

he claimed not to have understood any of it because his own English was so poor.

Nonetheless, my forefather spoke for some time, seriously, earnestly, just the way a grandfather would speak to his grandchild. And just as someone very young will pretend to understand the instructions of someone much older, I nodded my head as though comprehending.

The shaman was trying so hard that I wanted her to succeed, and that meant believing in this conjured ghost from my purported past. She was now sweating heavily; her lips were twitching, and as the spirit spoke his English, her hands trembled, her arms seemed no longer under her control. The spirit was taking over. So she suddenly sat down, this large woman, then fell backward, full length at my feet, eyes closed, mouth still, the spirit just as suddenly fled.

When she opened her eyes she seemed dazed, could remember nothing, then bit by bit her experience returned to her. A big fight, said my student interpreter, because it came from so far back and was so old, and the more old the more strong, very difficult to control.

Was he angry about something? No, just excited, talking to an ancestor like this. But she was sorry the connection got cut off. She was . . . Overloaded? Yes, overloaded. Too bad. I could have asked a question about the future.

She was sitting up now like a boxer after a knock-out, still groggy but game, and I wondered what kind of question about the future I could have asked. Nothing about myself, maybe something about her and her country. But I already knew the answer.

Any place this practical, this pragmatic, this concerned with the here and now and at the same time this curious about a past that had resulted in this present is as healthy as countries get—truncated, it will heal.

Then, reassured, I paid and went on my way to Kyongjiu.

YAP

The Island That Remained Itself

The Carolina archipelago of islands and atolls stretches below Guam and the Marianas. Yap is—along with Pohnpei and Chuuk (Truk)—one of them, now a member of these Federated States of Micronesia. It was first "discovered" by the Portuguese in 1526. The story goes that the visitors pointed and asked what these people called themselves. The native canoeists thought that the foreigners were pointing to their boats, so they held up their oars and said "Yap," which, in Yapese, means "oar."

Having thus established a lack of understanding, which can be said still to continue, Yap moved into the civilized world, or the other way around.

Though the foreigners characterized the Yapese as being "without malice, fear or cautiousness," they still moved in and went on trying to take over.

Despite their several attempts to defend their islands, the Yapese were next visited by the Spanish, then by the English, and were eventually colonized by the Germans. When WWI forced the German retreat, Japan took control and held Yap until it, too, lost a war. Though the U.S. forces did not actually invade the major island, some atolls became support bases from 1944 on. Now an independent state, Yap is still in close proximity to the U.S. bases in Guam, and its economy is based on U.S. dollars.

Nonetheless, or consequently, the Yapese, still lacking in both malice and fear, have been, among all the other Micronesian peoples, the most reluctant to adopt Western ways. Though there are plenty of T-shirts and track shoes, there are also grass skirts, toplessness, and loincloths. And there are no fast-food franchises from abroad—in great contrast to Guam, which is now mainly a mall purveying everything from Burger King to Bulgari.

A result is that Yap has much remained itself. Yap proper and its capital, Colonia, still have a "South Seas" appearance, with cargo ships in the harbor, one-story houses among the palms, and neon-lit bars that look as though Humphrey Bogart will be walking out any minute.

Among the reasons for this admirable refusal of the worst of our Western century is that Yap remains, in many senses, traditional. Though there is an elected state legislature, Yap's constitution also empowers two councils of traditional leaders—one consisting of chiefs from Yap proper, the other of chiefs from the outer islands.

These highly conservative bodies have the right to veto any legislation that affects traditional customs and, in the words of one local whom I asked, they "pretty much decide who runs and who wins in general elections."

The social structure of Yap—one based on a complex caste system—consequently remains intact. The village in which you are born determines both your name and your caste—though the rank within the caste may vary. Important as this strict differentiation is, it is not instantly visible. One cannot tell where a village stands in the caste hierarchy just by going there.

Indeed, one often cannot identify that it is a village. There are no adjacent households, except in Colonia. The entire population of Yap (about 12,000) is half in the capital, with the other half evenly dispersed elsewhere. A village is spread over the countryside, and each villager has whole hectares around him, every plot of which has a name and a rank. There is, consequently, no public land.

This affects the visitor. Just as you are expected to ask permission (and receive it) before you take a picture of a Yap person, so, too, once you step off the "municipal" stone-filled paths that criss-cross the island, you must ask to do so since you are about to step on someone's property. The permission is always given, but the asking indicates the degree of social construction that informs the Yap system.

This ancient order has been very effective in warding off the worst of the modern. There are no big resorts on Yap — nor small ones either. Getting permission to build on this land would be a formidable administrative task. There are no movie theaters, though there is TV; no pachinko (but some karaoke); no drugs, except, it is said, a bit of pot — and what might be called a national addiction to betel nut. There are also few hotels, all of them small, fewer restaurants, and no apparent prostitution.

It sounds like paradise, and in a way it is. In addition to freedom from pachinko and prostitution, there are no snakes, no poisonous insects, no crime on the streets — indeed, few streets. Rather, there is an abundance of seasonal fruits — mangoes, papayas, bananas, lemons, limes — a temperature that is always right (around 81°F), and not all that much rain.

Whether it is this paradisiacal for the Yapese is more open to question. Wages are low ($1 U.S. an hour for ordinary work), and many in the area have moved elsewhere (Guam, or the U.S.A.). In addition, there are typhoons. On Easter, April 2004, one hit Yap and caused much damage, including scooping out its best beach at Bechiyal and rendering for the time being inoperable its well-known cultural center.

But then beaches are not usually a big part of the Micronesian experience, though diving and snorkeling certainly are. One of the best spots for these is right off Bechiyal, where you can swim among the great manta rays, using the Yinbinaew Passage as a short cut to northern waters. Another attraction is sailing the mangrove forests, a labyrinth growing around the Tagreng Canal, viewable by small motor boats rented at the Colonia pier.

One more Yap experience is the village festival. In March there is the large annual event that brings music and dance from even the furthest atoll, but there are also local festivals all during the year, and the foreign visitor is invited if interest is shown.

Here grass skirts, loincloths, and toplessness are much in evidence, and songs and dances, ancient and modern, are rendered. One of the most popular is the "stick dance," in which the participants use bamboo poles to strike and counter. When I expressed interest, I was told that the dance is of fairly modern inspiration, being based upon the punishment methods adopted by the Japanese occupiers during WWII.

Told all this in English, too, since that is the lingua franca of Yap. There are three different dialects of Yapese, but these are so different that their speakers cannot understand each other—hence, by default, English. And American visitors can not only speak their own tongue but also spend their own currency.

The alternate currency of Yap, one rarely spent at all, is the famous *rai*, stone money, coins of which can range up to twelve feet) in diameter and weigh as much as five tons. It is kept outside in "banks" lined up along village pathways and is never moved, not even when ownership changes. The most valuable *rai* are not the largest but those that—being heavy—cost the most lives when ferried by canoe up from a quarry in far Palau.

It is one of the first things shown to the interested visitor, along with the village *faluw*, a large thatched structure that is the traditional community house. These are still used as meeting places for the village leaders, though traditionally they also served as schools for young boys and as quarters for bachelors. No longer common on Yap proper, though still seen on outlying atolls, is the *dapal*, where young girls were sent for instruction and where women were once put to wait out their menstrual periods.

Yap is thus a state where the traditional is still holding its own against the incursions of the contemporary. It has only fairly recently been "opened" (there are fewer than a hundred "visitor rooms" in the entire archipelago) and is still refreshingly lacking in those depredations that are said to attract tourists. Hotels are simple, basic, restaurants are few but good once you find them, and it is a pleasure to be with a proud people still without fear or malice, who somehow remain unaffected by the West and its ways.

JAPAN

The Stone Garden of Ryoan-ji

A rectangle of fifteen stones set in white gravel, surrounded on three sides by a low wall, on the fourth by a viewing veranda, a green grove rising above the low wall—the stone garden of Kyoto's Ryoan-ji, no larger than a backyard, possesses by its nature an inability to change.

The sun may shine or not, there may be rain or snow, the trees outside turn green, brown, black, the seasons pass, but the garden reveals no difference. It has its own time, its own season. It is immutable.

Like the ancient pyramids, it is always the same, but unlike the pyramids it does not proclaim this. Hidden away in a corner of a temple off in the suburbs of a city, it has the value of a whisper in a world of shouts. I enter the temple, turn a corner, walk along a corridor, and suddenly there it is—precisely as it was when I last saw it, just as seen when new.

That this should be consoling is an evaluation. Since the garden does not change and since its aspect is forever the same, it becomes something to be relied upon. It gives rest and peace and demands nothing. Friends die, empires fall, but it remains. You might see it in youth, in middle age, when old—and it would be the single sight that remained the same. You would have changed, but not it.

Your thoughts on the garden would have changed as well. At first, perhaps, you saw, like a child, black islands in a white sea. Later, adolescent, you would discover another explanation—it is really a mother tiger and her young crossing a river. Later, more mature, you would see that the garden is not an anecdote.

I then thought of mathematics, astronomy, music, and the garden turned abstract, the living blueprint of a garden, a kind of happening in stones and gravel, meaningful only in its permanence. Then, now older, I look at the garden and wonder: Don't those rocks look like black islands in a white sea?

A few other things in life do not change, though ideas about them do. Mozart delights when young and saddens when old, but the music is the same. Beethoven cannot do this, because Beethoven is usually about something and Mozart rarely is. The Vatican, the Great Wall of China, Nikko—they are all about something, but the stone garden isn't. It has no priorities, no ambitions, no intentions, and, because it does not demand, it captivates.

It is enigmatic. There is no order in the fifteen stones—they were put the way they are because they looked right that way. The stones and the white gravel are but tools that serve the idea of a garden made of them alone. They commemorate this extraordinary notion. The garden would be just as successful if the stones were in different positions, if the stones were white and the gravel black.

They are the remnants of an original vision. It is a remarkable one—a stone garden is a contradiction in terms. But this is because it is what is left of a vision, and it thus demands attention.

I remember looking at the moon when I was 18. It was just before I was, for the first time, leaving the country where I had been born and, feeling this emotion, I looked at the full moon over that Atlantic beach and thought: I am seeing the moon, I am looking at it, I shall not forget what it looks like.

The sight of the moon is common. Once a month it seems full, and it is usually available someplace in the sky. Yet it is enigmatic. It appears to change and yet it is always the same. Our eyes are drawn to it. All over the world, at this very instant, people in wholly different countries are saying: Oh, look at the moon.

And from that ocean beach I looked into the future as well and imagined myself in different places, looking at the full moon, and remembering this first time. And I have indeed often stopped and looked: from the Acropolis, at a Chiang Mai wat, in darkened Dubrovnik — each time myself older.

Each time I thought back to the younger moon along the Atlantic, memories of these more exotic moons vanished. I thought: It hasn't changed. I've changed and it hasn't. And it was with pleasure that I understood this.

This, the moon and a few other things give us — Delphi, Mozart's string quartets, the stone garden. They offer the feeling of serenity that comes from the acceptance of inner change when presented with outer immutability, the pleasure that acknowledging transience gives, the quiet joy of knowing evanescence.

These things have the power to compel return. For one who has once been to Ryoan-ji, it is nearly impossible not to go once more. It is an imperative. It becomes necessary to go again to the garden—to find out, as it were.

This should not be confused with pleasure. Visiting the garden for the first time is a pleasure, for it is extremely beautiful. At the same time it is disquieting, because one can find no reason for the beauty. Second, third, fourth visits occur. And they are replicas of the first. One brings only memories of former visits, one can bring nothing else. And the garden offers nothing at all—it just stands there, eternal, unchanging, and, yes, beautiful.

There is, then, only one way to sit on the wooden veranda in front of this collection of stones and gravel. Sit there and remember the other times. And you achieve serenity. No, you achieve nothing—serenity is forced upon you. Otherwise you leave.

In this way the unchanging garden gives knowledge of change. I feel it deeply, painfully. I cannot forget the other times, I must be aware of them and of myself, both then and now. Usually in life you may stifle this awareness. But here you cannot. You must wrestle and win and stay, or lose and go.

The garden cannot help being stern—even its beauty is austere. The style is consistent, though, and this means honesty. It must be trusted completely or not at all. No one can be half-involved with Ryoan-ji. It would be the same as being half-involved with yourself.

This stone garden is a moral object. It never answers questions, it only—like a sphinx—asks them. Consequently it attracts, and since we cannot know what it seems to be asking, we can only draw near, and visit it again and again.

This is sufficient. We cannot know what the garden is about, but we dimly, fleetingly understand what we are.

The Sacred Heights of Koya-san

Koya is a temple city atop a forested mountain in the Wakayama ranges south of Osaka. It is the original center of the Shingon sect of Buddhism, and still offers the willing pilgrim a religious experience.

The compound was established in 816 by the priest Kukai, who had studied in far China. When he returned he opened the first ecclesiastical school devoted to Shingon Mikkyo (Esoteric Buddhism), the Tantric religion that worships Dainichi Nyorai, the Japanese name for the being who predates the Shakyamuni Buddha himself.

The school flourished. Shingon spread, and Koya-san became a Lhasa-like place of pilgrimage. It still is, even though Koya-cho, the town center, now holds—in addition to its more than 120 temples—tour buses, coffee shops, and pachinko parlors.

There is Kongobu-ji, with its decorated doors illustrating scenes from Kukai's life; the Konpon Daito, an enormous central pagoda, said to have been designed by Kukai himself; the Danjo Garden, where Kukai had his original school; and the beautifully simple Meido, Kukai's residence, where he died while meditating.

He still meditates, now in the Gobyo, a mausoleum, deep in the surrounding forest. He was taken there, still in the cross-legged meditative position, and there he remains, say the faithful, awaiting the coming of the Buddha. He has a new name as well as a new address. His posthumous title is Kobo Daishi, and he is a Buddhist saint, known affectionately as Odaishi-sama by the faithful pilgrims.

One sees these everywhere at Koya-san—some one and a half million come yearly, many of them wearing white coats with *dogyo ninin* (two-person group) printed on them, signifying that each is making a pilgrimage accompanied by Odaishi-sama himself.

Every morning, early, the pilgrims stream through the town, setting out on their pilgrimage past the Tibetan-looking temples and the Los Angeles–looking parking lots. The road leads directly toward an enormous cryptomeria forest—and then suddenly stops. We have come to the end of our century.

There is a great gate and a small bridge, Ichinohashi, to make an exit from our prosaic present, to mark the entrance into the sacred past. Here begins the forest and the narrow paved walk that meanders on among the massive trees.

Across the bridge and under the gate, there is sudden quiet. It descends like a balm. Only now do I realize how irreverently noisy the temple town was. Among the trees the only sound is the dropping of water and the shuffle of the pilgrims' straw sandals. We walk deeper into the dappled forest. The air grows cooler, more moist. At one side looms the first, the great stone burial stupas.

This is medieval Japan, a somber place, all greens and earth-colors suddenly rent by the scarlet of a funeral flag. And here, lining the path as I wander ever deeper, are the people of the past—the illustrious dead. Known by us or not, the names are carved deep into the stone—Toyotomi Hideyoshi, Oda Nobunaga—here perhaps lie these famous heroes and villains, disguised now by their posthumous titles. Plus hundreds of the now-forgotten. And what does this path, these tombs, those towering trees, remind one of? Yes, of course, a cathedral.

Through the standing cypress columns, under the great windows of the dawn-struck pines, the path leads past the Nokosudo, where rest the ashes of centuries of devotees, and the Torodo, the low-eaved temple where hang 3,000 lanterns, kept burning night and day. Some of them, it is said, have been burning since they were first lit a thousand years ago. And here, every morning, are held the fire rituals that mark this branch of the Shingon sect.

From a distance I hear the sounds of gongs and drums. Now, as I draw nearer, I sense the mighty ground-bass of the monks chanting their sutras. The sun appears and is greeted with fire and the smoke of incense. Through the scented haze, new sunlight pierces the dark temple hall and the brass gongs flow.

By the altar there is the pulsing light of coals and the scent of the powdered incense poured upon them. Clouds of smoke roil to the ceiling and rise through the standing trees into the brightening sky. The drums pound and the priests chant a greeting to the sun.

This music is also heard, it is said, by Kobo Daishi himself, who meditates nearby. He is not asleep, much less dead, and for over a thousand years he has heard this daily service, which he himself originated.

His mausoleum, if it can so be called, is set at an angle facing into the deep woods. It is so old that its roof is covered with brilliant forest-green moss. Here sits the still-living saint, meditating on.

One believes this, or at least one wants to. The forested graveyard of Koya-san, with its brilliant inner temples and the moss-green resting place of the saint—all of this weaves an experience that must be termed religious, that calls out for belief.

In this sanctity the common self drops away. I realize that I am not enough, that I need assistance, and that this is what religions offer. My leaning toward assistance is my first step toward faith.

Actually, however, my steps are already carrying me out of this mystical outdoor cathedral and back into the everyday world I inhabit. I turn my back on the green-moss hut where sits the saint. The last scent of incense is replaced by the first of bus exhaust.

But this is enough—this escape into the past, into an age where faith was possible. The visit revives. It awakes a sense of wonder long left dormant. The memory of sanctity remains. All the way through the now Disneyland-looking town, all the way down the cool mountain, out onto the hot plain, all the way back to the city.

The Lakes of Hokkaido

Walking along the forested shores of the Go-ko, the five lakes of the Shiretoko Peninsula in the far northeast of

Hokkaido, Japan's most northern island, I turn a wooded point and there, lined up, is a whole family of foxes.

Father, mother, two almost-grown cubs—they are waiting to see the tourists. The lakes have so recently been opened up and the visitors are yet so few that the animals are still taken with the novelty.

We tourists are entranced as well, and not only by the waiting fox family. There is the beauty of nature as yet unbruised, a sense of huge space, a lingering scent of wildness—all qualities not usually associated with Japan.

The finger of land pointing from the corner of Hokkaido is still frontier—Japan's last. Its name, Shiretoko, is an Ainu word used by those aboriginals to mean "the end of the earth," and so it is. Here the land stops and the widest ocean in the world begins.

Main-island Japanese visiting Hokkaido seem to think that they are in a foreign country—which in a way they are. The island has been settled only since the last century, and the forces shaping it were those of nineteenth-century Meiji Japan—not those of the medieval Tokugawa era.

The architecture, for example, is not Japanese in any traditional sense. It is all clapboard, with many barns and silos. Long, cold winters have made Hokkaido much more like Siberia or Canada than the Japan of which it is a part.

There are still great stands of white birch, spruce, and pine, but the only bamboo seen is the ubiquitous bamboo grass. In Shiretoko itself there are forests of oak, plains of juniper, hot waterfalls, a volcano erupting pure sulfur, and the still-pristine five lakes upon whose shores I now stand.

These little lakes are at the very edge of a precipice that

falls away to the Sea of Okhotsk six hundred feet below. All five of them teem with trout-like *masu*, and the forest extends to the very lip of these shores. Now a narrow path has been cut that winds its way among them. Some four miles in all, the course takes an hour or two, and the foxes come early to get the best seats.

For how long, I wonder—in the summer whole busloads will come from Iwaobetsu Spa down the coast. Still, northeastern Hokkaido has been conscientious about protecting itself. Enormous stretches are designated as national parks, "developers" are actively discouraged, and except for the highways winding through the mountains, the land remains much as it has always been.

Lake Mashu, for example, far south of Shiretoko—and, I should imagine, one of the most beautiful lakes in the world— is well guarded. The tourist is forced to keep a distance—a caldera lake, its walls are so steep that descent is dangerous, and in any event forbidden. It may be regarded only from two lookout points, both of which are located well above its untroubled surface.

Climbing to one of the lookout points, I view spreading beneath me something I never thought I'd see in this crowded and polluted archipelago—mile upon mile of unbroken and primordial forest surrounding this lake of the purest and most crystalline blue. There was not a cabin, not a boat, not a trashcan, not a tourist.

Descending from these heights, I stopped to look at neighboring Kussharo, the largest lake in Hokkaido. It is cobalt, an odd shade for a lake but indicative of a high mineral content. This water, I am told, is bad for fish but good for skin. As a consequence, it does not teem with piscine life as do other Hokkaido lakes.

Nor is it so well protected. Kussharo's southern extremity already offers a beach, tents, hostels, garbage. Also, touristed-up, it offers a stuffed bear to be photographed with—and a live Ainu.

The Ainu, the original inhabitants of Hokkaido and northern Honshu, no longer hunt or fish. They are pressed into the tourist trade—weaving, carving, posing. A handsome, quiet people, they are slowly going the way of the sightseeing foxes.

There are few pristine places left them—the small lakes of Penketo and Panketo, perhaps. One, Lake Onnato, is so secluded that we are not even given a glimpse. Such corners, however, offer little to a people no longer allowed to hunt or to trap. Yet, these lakes lie on old Ainu land, as their names proclaim. These are not Japanese names—main-island tourists cannot even properly read the Ainu name of the main Abashiri airport: Memonbetsu.

There is a whole Ainu "village" on the southern shore of the most famous of the Hokkaido northeast lakes, Akan. Though there is some carving and lots of posing there, too, one can at least visit these people in something approaching a noncommercial venue and observe whatever way of life is left.

The Ainu hunted and fished, but they were not despoilers. It is doubtful that any people ever lived more amicably with nature. Even their religion, a form of animism, was benign. This spirit still exists in Akan, though tourist boats now cross the deep blue waters and tourist buses go up the two sacred mountains, O-Akan and Me-Akan. Nonetheless, once out on the lake or up in the mountains, one is in spirit returned to a natural world.

The waters of Lake Akan are home to the fabled *marimo*, those globe-shaped balls of algae that rise in the shallows and fall in the depths, as though intelligent. They are ancient — marimo the size of baseballs can be two hundred years old, and there are some that are a yard across. The Ainu worshiped them, and one understands why.

So, despite the tourist toehold, something remains pristine. Surprising to foreign tourists and amazing to the Japanese, it is still a land where foxes go sightseeing, where trout winnow the waters, where the mysterious marimo glide up from the depths.

The Satsuma Peninsula

The southern tip of the most southern island of Japan, the Satsuma Peninsula is also the furthest west. It was here that the first Westerners landed. The Dutch arrived, bringing the Batavian sweet potato, the Portuguese came toting firearms, and in 1549 Francis Xavier came bearing the gospel.

By the time he departed, the future saint had formed the highest opinion of the place. "Judging by the people," he said, "the Japanese are the best race yet discovered. . . . They are very sociable, usually good and not malicious, and much concerned with their honor, which they prize above everything else."

It was the people of Satsuma that Francis was talking

about, and even now they maintain their fine reputation. They are (besides everything the Jesuit said they were) also expansive, open, gregarious, impulsive, and opinionated—all qualities that, no matter how admirable, are not immediately associated with the rest of the Japanese.

Reasons for this are sometimes suggested. An expansive man beside me in the sake shop thought it was because of the sweet potato, locally called the Satsuma-*imo*. "We make this drink out of it, *imo-shochu*, which is so strong it just naturally keeps us in good spirits. Like to try some?"

On the other hand, a woman schoolteacher on the bus told me: "I think it's our natural environment. It's still natural, you see. Oh, we have our oil refineries, up near Kagoshima City, but down here we're natural. And it's so beautiful."

Indeed it is, one of the most beautiful places in Japan, with its low-lying volcanic hills and long plateaus. There is a perfectly triangular mountain, Kaimondake, a splendidly crenulated coast, and, in season, waves of pinkish cherry blossoms decorating the hills, and blankets of bright yellow *nanohana* blossoms covering the plains.

And it is warm. Satsuma is far south, on a parallel with New Orleans. Though February can be chilly, the rest of the months are mild. Tea grows year-round, and there are all sorts of citrus, including that small, sweet, fragrant mandarin, the Satsuma *mikan*.

"No, no, no," said the opinionated high-school principal at Ibusuki when I modestly offered as my own some of these theories as to the origin of the excellence of the Satsuma people. "It is simply that we were spared the worst of the military government that the rest of the country had to put up with for all of those centuries. You find in us the kind of people *all* Japanese once were — before the Tokugawas."

The Tokugawa family unified Japan back in the sixteenth century, but it did so only by establishing something like a police state. "Spies everywhere. That was when people learned to be tight-mouthed, suspicious. Spies! Even in the toilet!"

The toilet? I asked, and he told me to go to Chiran if I didn't believe him. So I went to Chiran, in the middle of the peninsula, the most extensive area of preserved samurai dwellings anywhere in Japan.

Stone walls, thick, clipped hedges, severe traditional gardens, and toilets built right into the gates. Upon inquiry I learned that these were said to have been for the convenience of guests, but that they also permitted the squatting samurai to eavesdrop on conversations outside.

I looked into one of them, a cold and comfortless place. From the latticed window I listened to a group of Japanese tourists passing and quite clearly heard their conversation. "Gucci's still all right," one of them was saying, "but up in Osaka now Vuitton's more popular."

These closed and claustrophobic lanes seemed the only cold place in the peninsula that sunny day. Ostentatious, chilly little gardens, and forcibly espaliered *kantsubaki* — winter camellia, that pale blossom long loved by the Japanese military because when it falls it does so with a thud, just like a head when it is cut off.

Nevertheless, though redolent of military manipulations, Chiran was a small place. It had in no way controlled the province of Satsuma as similar cold garrisons had once con-

Back to the question of reasons for the sterling qualities of Satsuma, the waiter at the Kantsubaki Koffee Korner
in downtown Kagoshima, overlooking Sakurajima, with its
smoking volcano, said: "It might have been the Chinese influence—they've been coming for centuries, and they are a lot
more expansive than we are."

This is true. Satsuma is where prewar rich Chinese used
to come for vacation and to endure the hot baths of Ibusuki.
Now they are, I am told, returning. The spas of Satsuma had
been for the better-off postwar Japanese, but now they are
for the Chinese—and the Koreans as well.

"Used to be that the Kanko was filled with Japanese on
their honeymoons. Now they all go to Hawaii and it's the Korean honeymooners who fill it up. And," the garrulous waiter
continued, indicating yet another demographic change, "I
hear that they're going to tear it all down anyway and make a
kurhaus for old folks."

Among all these theories attempting to account for the
fine people of Satsuma, I best like the historical one. History
keeps culture alive, I decided, and said as much to the con-
ductor while being bussed up over the spectacular Ibusuki
Skyline Highway, looking back over where I had been—baby
Fuji, monster lake, big white Kanko small in the distance.

"Why, even Urashima Taro is still remembered," I said.
"Satsuma is really where he came from."

"Maybe," she said, "but I'm from Miyazaki [rival Kyushu
city], and our Aoshima is actually where he started out." She
smiled with native pride. "We got the Princess Shrine there
and the turtle he rode on, or one like it, stuffed."

The Shores of the Noto Hanto

The Noto Hanto, that peninsula stretching into the Sea of Japan, a large hook of land worked by the waves on its outer edge, indented with bays and coverts on its inner, is even now a hinterland. Elongating into the sea, it has the simplicity of an island, a landscape composed only of itself. As in a child's coloring book, one expects the parts to be labeled: The Bay, The Mountain, The Port.

This is also the simplicity of old Japan, a country not then rich enough to have been able to afford clutter. Almost everything was used, little was thrown away. The result was a landscape composed only of its own salient elements. As in the land, so in the habitations. The farmhouses, many of them still thatched, plainly show their structure: The House, The Roof, The Door.

There is also the simplicity of a cold country, something which the sprawling and indulgent south does not know. Here everything is compact, turned in upon itself, for warmth, as it were. Everything is of some use.

❀

Rain. I look from the dripping window of the train to Wajima, gaze at the misty forests. The trees are conifers, indicating how cold it gets in the winter, how cool it remains in the summer.

After a few civil remarks, the old country woman sitting on her feet beside me looks from the window and says: "Rain again. It often rains in Noto. But, you know, it is on days like that that you are given the real feel of the place." The real feel of Japan. How often is one offered this? —something distilled over the centuries: patterns, ideas, attitude, still maintained.

❖

A cool, slow evening along the *sotoura*, the rugged outer coast, high cliffs, dark now, filled with caves, festooned with waterfalls. Then, from the far-off lights of Sosogi, the distant drums. The demons have come.

There, in a small shrine on a hillside, they stand—demons all. One beats a continual, rapid, staccato tattoo, while the others, one after another, strike poses, sticks aloft, then leap and turn to batter the great drum, the rhythm accelerating, arms flexing, sweat scattering, masks glowing with ferocity in the torchlight. The audience—farmers, their wives, child—draw back as though afraid.

But the demons are farmers, too, amateurs who keep alive this old ritual of the demon drummers of Noto. Long ago, in medieval civil wars, the encroaching troops of the shogun pushed this far into the hinterland. Fearful of the incursion, the farmers invented a stratagem. Suddenly, at night, in front of the advancing soldiers would leap into torchlight a band of ferocious demons, menacing, beating their infernal tattoo. The soldiers, just as superstitious as the farmers themselves, would beat a confused retreat.

So goes the story and, indeed, the shogun's forces never did settle the peninsula, and even now the folk of the Noto Hanto display an individuality said to be denied conquered, neighboring provinces.

Now the rhythms climb and leap, the flames of the torch-
es billow and crackle—a final cacophony, a fierce tableau,
and the performance is over. Masks are removed, revealing
country faces, sweat-covered, smiling, acknowledging the
applause. And yet, for the moment, the ferocity of old Noto
had been there before us in these *gojinjo-daiko*.

*

In Japan you can always tell where you are by looking
at the roofs. In each district of the country they are different. Here in Noto they are, when not thatched, a typical and
intricate arrangement of black tiles set in three tiers so as to
break the weight of the winter snows. These are elegant, even
delicate-looking structures, soaring up, appearing so fragile
that one wonders if they would deflect even the rain.

It was beneath one of these elegant roofs that a farmer
told me what the name Noto means. I had stopped at his
farmhouse in Suzu for a glass of water. The place is so famous
for its natural, pure water—all the people here are pleased to
share this liquid so delicious that it becomes a beverage.

"They tell you all sorts of things, these professor types,"
said the farmer after I had drunk his water. "But you take it
from me, Noto is an Ainu word. Yes, those people used to live
this far west. It was *nopo* and it meant *hanareta*—set apart."

Set apart, that is what *nopo* means, and Noto is more set
apart than anywhere else in Japan. "But don't pay attention
to the way that they write Noto now. Now they have it that
the *no* means 'bear' and the *to* means 'climbing,' and I sup-
pose the idea of a bear climbing does give the idea of some

set-apart place, but that is just the doings of those professor fellows. You just remember the Ainu. They got it right."

*

Around the cape, down inside the peninsula, the *uchiura*, a coast of inlets and coves, spotted with tiny wooded islands, all looking like the designs on old plates, picturesque and somehow domesticated . . . and then, standing straight from its shallow bay, the amazing island of Mitsuke.

It stands straight from the sea, high cliffs surrounded by forest, the landward edge forming a great prow. This appearance accounts for the local name — Battleship Island — while the proper name indicates that it was "found" (*mitsukaru*).

This finding could not have been a difficult feat. How could you miss it? But it was "found" by that great early traveler, the medieval monk Kobo Daishi, and so it was memorialized.

Indeed, if you find anything extraordinary at all in Japan, you may be certain that Kobo Daishi is lurking somewhere behind it. As for this island, the learned monk, also Japan's first tourist, would have been pleased at its success. Mitsukejima is a local attraction, and many bathe alongside in the shallow bay. Its sheer size and unexpected beauty quite dwarf the vacationers. They look featureless, like the small beings in the prints of Hiroshige who are there not as individuals but as yet another aspect of nature.

*

Inland is Yanagida, a mountain village famous for its lacquer. So is most of Noto, to be sure, but here is something special: a storehouse, the immense interior of which is composed entirely of lacquer-work.

Walls, floors, ceiling, everything—it is like being in an enormous art deco jewel box, all modern red and black, Mondrian geometric, but huge. Lacquer is so expensive that even a small box is precious. Here, however, is this vast room.

I attempt to discover why it was so constructed. Sitting around the open hearth with the last of the Nakatanis, now a portly gentleman, I ask. "Well," comes the reply, "there are several reasons." One certainly was the wish to be ostentatious. But another might have been the great economic depression of over three centuries ago, when the lord wanted to give occupation to otherwise idle craftsmen.

"Not like today," he says, then unexpectedly adds: "Now that we've got robots. Soon there won't be anything but robots. No more lacquer, of course. Robots can't make lacquer." Then, in explanation: "They're all around—young robots. They don't read anything but comic books and they perm their hair and they can't think. Robots already—that's what they are."

Having disposed of the younger generation of citified Japanese, we drink our tea in that agreeable silence left when undoubted truths have been voiced.

*

Achingly picturesque, this *uchiura*—as at Tsukumo (Ninety-nine Inlets) Bay, one small wooded island after another, receding into the distance, veiled by twilight, still touched by the setting sun. The hotel at Ogi is high atop one of these islands. From it one descends (by elevator, this being Japan) to the waterside pavilion for supper.

The food in Ishikawa Prefecture is famous, but in Noto even this standard of excellence is surpassed. All the food is local, from the sea or from the mountains, all of it is seasonal, and all is prepared in the Noto manner.

Supper consists of fresh shrimp, squid boiled with *miso* bean paste, sea trout in foil with *yuzu* peel, fresh *tanbu* shellfish, baby octopus and marinated mountain potatoes, grilled *buri* (yellow tail), spider crabs (two feet across) grilled on fresh conifer, aubergine marinated with peppers, *sazae* wreath-shell cooked over charcoal, a *suimono* soup of tidal clams, white rice, all this followed by fresh grapes, and all of it enjoyed with the local sake, followed by the local tea and, very shortly afterward, by sleep.

✿

On the way back down the inner coast, the man next to me, carrying on his lap a great hamper of fresh sea urchins, asks if my country, too, has four seasons. The Japanese are unable to believe that any other place has four separate and distinct seasons. They think only Japan does. I used to be a bit impatient with this question, but no longer.

Looking at this man with his gnarled hands and weathered face, I see in him someone created by these seasons. It is not that Japan is the only country to have seasons—it is the only country to live with them.

And so I answer that, yes, my country has four seasons, but that they are nothing like Japan's. And they aren't, because no one makes anything of them.

Pleased at this news, the old man settles back for a talk. "Our winters," he begins, "are long and hard. . . ."

Kunisaki — Land's End

One corner of Kyushu, the southernmost island of Japan, remains mysterious — the Kunisaki Peninsula. Well-known Fukuoka, the southern metropolis, is to the north; Beppu, famous tourist spa, is to the southeast; but Kunisaki remains a land of ancient woods and hidden valleys, folded mountains and history visible. Land's End, that is what I am told the name means, and it seems to fit — where the known stops, where myth begins.

For example, just what vanished civilization would have left, deep in the mountains, the Kumano Magaibutsu? These are enormous bas-reliefs carved into the natural rock face of an inner peak; the largest of their kind in Japan, the carvings — the Dainichi Nyorai Buddha and the Fudo Myo-o — tower in this wilderness, cut with enormous effort and for no known reason.

These are, even now in this age of tourism, difficult to reach. When I eventually located the defile leading into the gorge, I was handed an alpenstock. *Whatever for?* I wondered, but soon discovered. Up and up I toiled, sweating in the morning sun, my stick biting into soft moss, slipping on smooth stone.

After half an hour, tired, thirsty, I met some descending pilgrims and asked how much further. "Oh," said one of them, "you're not even close." And so I wasn't, for it was not until much later that finally, deep in the dim forest, I found the beginning.

I was at the bottom of a titanic staircase made of massive stones that led straight up the mountain. The end was so distant I could not see it. Whoever could have made it?

"The demons," said an old women, carefully pouring herself tea from her thermos. "They built it—and all in one night." But those are gods up there, so why had the demons done that? "The gods made them do it," was the firm reply as the top of the thermos was screwed on tight. "So they made it in a hurry."

It took me another hour of climbing, resting on one mighty and arbitrary slab after another, until, properly panting, I stood under the regard of the gods. There they were, enormous, carved into the rock a thousand years ago.

"At least that's the date that's been decided on," said the bespectacled priest at the small shrine perched nearby. "Late tenth century—Heian period." But by whom, I wanted to know. So he told me another theory.

The people who lived here were from Korea, and they had long lived in Kunisaki. But a thousand years ago the Yamato tribe—the Japanese—descended into Kyushu from the Honshu homeland and drove them out. But which side, Korean or Yamato, had carved these, I wanted to know, looking up into Buddha's great all-seeing eye. "*Saaa,*" said the shrine-keeper. "Which, I wonder."

This is a land about which everyone wonders. Though

only 12.5 miles across and but half an hour's drive from the Oita Airport, it remains as though forgotten—filled with thatched-roofed farmhouses, with hamlets still using wells, with country roads and the kind of comfortable rustic scenery once so common and now so rare.

And there is not much about it in the guidebooks, though there are still a number of historical remains in Kunisaki. "But not nearly so many as there once were," said a local history teacher I met at the single general store, sitting at a crossroads with a shrine, a bus stop, and a phone booth.

"There was this local lord—Atomo Sori by name. He was a Christian, and so he went around knocking down whatever he found. Heathen remains, he called them. But he couldn't get at the big carvings, and there are a couple of temples he missed, too. Here, I'll show you where they are."

He marked the map I had bought at the airport, and in this way I discovered the lovely Fuki-ji, a beautiful, eleventh-century temple. Its timber had long since slivered, and it was sitting all by itself (no fences, no loudspeakers, no tourist buses), looking as it had probably always looked.

Inside the temple there was a wooden image of Amida— the Buddha in one of his more pensive incarnations. And, behind him, festivities in the pure land he promised, painted on wood centuries ago and now spotted white—a leprous paradise.

There was just me and the caretaker, a young woman knitting a scarlet muffler. I asked if it was Heian period. She stopped, counted her stitches, then said: "Fujiwara."

So, the mighty Fujiwara family had come here, too, presumably after quelling the local Koreans. And I remembered other remains elsewhere—the big Fujiwara complex up in Hiraizumi, now all under glass, encased in a concrete shell, filled with shuffling schoolchildren, and dead, dead, dead. And here in this open, rolling countryside was a perfect Fujiwara temple, silver with age, lying open on the land, breathing.

I thanked the knitting caretaker. "Forty-six, forty-seven," she said, then: "If you take the road to the left, in about half an hour you'll reach Futago-ji. Very nice, if you like that sort of thing."

Eventually I reached a large temple, built like a country house, with a veranda overlooking the verdant Futago valley. The steps were flanked with stone images of the fierce Nio-sama, guardians of the Buddha. But it was all new, said the young priest. Eighteenth century, in fact. All except for what was in the cave. And what was in the cave? "Go and see—no one knows how old it is."

In the darkness of the cave cut into the cliff behind the temple, illuminated by my single candle, something large squatted, something either fully dressed or else enormously fat. It had eyes, and they looked as though longingly at the patch of daylight that was the distant door. It was not the Buddha. It was rounder, heavier, older.

Once out I asked the young priest what it was. "Saaa— we just call him our *kamisama*, our local god."

But didn't anyone know? Maybe it was some dark Korean deity, ready to pounce. "Well, could be. Couple of teachers came down from the university last year to look at it, but they only came once. Anyway, we don't pay much attention to it. We live here," he concluded, as though that explained everything.

The sun slid to one side of the valley as I descended into the lower woods. It was dark between the trees—quite dark, unnaturally so, as though black crepe had been strung between the cedars, looped as though for some sinister purpose—a secret funeral in the forest.

I moved closer into the shadows and saw that it actually was black net, a course scrim, and in front of it were two old women wearing straw bonnets, eating rice balls, drinking their afternoon tea.

Did someone die? I wanted to know. Why was the forest all draped in black? Is it a funeral?

They laughed. "No, no," said one. "That's just to make it dark enough to grow *shiitake* mushrooms on the logs inside. Funeral!"

I stared into the dark forest, and the late sun slid behind the mountains. I thought about mysteries and black-draped woods, and—"Bats," said the other old woman. "Like a bat's ear, they say."

What was like a bat's ear?

"The shape. Kunisaki. The peninsula. Small, round, just like a bat's ear. Bats have ears, you know. Little ones."

Walking down the road to the bus stop, the sun now nearly gone, the forests truly black, I stopped at a small store—saws, ropes, pulleys, rice cakes.

"Going down to Beppu?" asked the man. "Been seeing the sights?"

I said that indeed I had and that I now understood why the peninsula was called Land's End.

"Land's what?"

"Land's End—that's what Kunisaki means."

"It does? That definition sounds a little suspicious."

I looked up, as the last sunlight caught the final mountains. "But that's what the lady at the airport said this morning, and if it doesn't mean that, what does it mean?"

"*Saa,*" he said and smiled. "I wonder."

Asakusa

In 1947 there was only one subway line in Tokyo, compared with the thirteen now operating, but its glorious terminus was Asakusa, then Japan's place to play—to Tokyo what Montmartre had been to Paris, what Times Square was to New York. This major entertainment district was described in a popular song of the day. "Asakusa is a human market/Asakusa is Tokyo's heart." It was a whole community of shows and shops, bars and brothels, with everything for sale—in particular, matters of the heart.

One spring day that year, I had hesitatingly stepped into the Ginza subway station, Asakusa-bound. Hesitatingly because the subway was off-limits to members of the Allied Occupation of Japan. There were still signs reading NO FRATERNIZATION WITH THE INDIGENOUS PERSONNEL. Since I was an occupier, an alert MP could have me sent back to Ohio for good. Once in the subway, however—once I had burrowed into the then-pervasive smell of old clothes and pickled radishes—there were no MPs.

And none in Asakusa either, though just about everything there was off-limits. I could wander at will, the only foreigner in the place, a covert occupier among the oblivious occupied, a single person gloriously lost in the pleasure-park crowds of a devastated city.

There was the Rokku, a solid street of motion-picture theaters, the first of which, the Denkikan, had opened in 1903. And the promenade along the Sumida River, where pretty girls with open parasols still stared. And the Naka-mise, that long row of roofed shops stretching from the Kaminari Gate, with its muscled guardian deities and its enormous hanging lantern, all the way to Senso-ji, the Asakusa Kannon temple.

At least it would have reached that far had the temple not been destroyed during the U.S. incendiary raids of March 9 and 10, 1945. Between 70,000 and 80,000 people were killed in these bombings, and some two-fifths of the city was razed, including most of Asakusa and all of Kannon's temple.

Yet now, less than two years later, the enterprise, the vitality of the place again overflowed. New shops and stalls, still smelling of sawdust, lined the alleys. Hundreds strolled, picking over the merchandise, loafing on the corners. All of them were out on a weekday for a good time, all dressed up (the single good kimono, the white shirt and tie) or down (army uniforms, farming garb); everyone out of fashion because they were still dressed for war and we were now well into peace. And everyone was smiling — there was possibility, prospects, the worst was over.

Lots of new entertainment, too. There was the tightrope strip-show, air-gun shooting galleries with packs of Golden Bat cigarettes as prizes, a new aquarium comprised of those denizens not eaten during the war years. The famous merry-go-round ("Japan's Largest") was back, though the Casino

Folies (next door), where the Asakusa Opera had been, was still a burned-out lot.

There were lots of such lots—where something had been, the holes not yet filled in. Buildings grouped around the gashes stood clumsy, as though apologetic. Particularly around the big crater that had been home of the Asakusa Opera, beloved by many, including the writers Yasunari Kawabata and Kafu Nagai, and remembered for its truncated *Rigoletto*, where "La Donna é Mobile" became a local hit even though, with no tenor available, the Duke had turned into a soprano.

Usually, however, the fare was varied. There were Charlie Chaplin imitators, comedy skits, and an all-girl dancing troupe, the popularity of which was occasioned, said the resident comedian, Enoken, by the completely false rumor that the girls dropped their drawers during Friday matinees.

Nagai remembered (in Edward Seidensticker's translation) what it was like backstage at the Asakusa Opera. "The powerful flesh of the arms and legs . . . called to mind the earthen hallway of a florist's shop, where a litter of torn-off petals and withering leaves is left unswept and trampled into shapelessness."

It was in this packed, gaudy, sexy, meretricious, and completely enchanting place that I wandered, along with so many others, happy to be pushed off the sidewalk as I stopped to sample roasted eel, a purported aphrodisiac, or peered into the back rooms and was stared back at by the resident courtesans, country girls bewigged, sandled, expensive. Or I could walk into the Tokyo Club Theatre and improve my knowledge of Japanese film.

Here in Asakusa was a reality that my Occupation round

of billet, office, and PX could not equal. So, from the first, I, no less than Kawabata or Nagai, became a devotee of Asakusa, a round-eyed flâneur on the narrow Asakusa boulevards. I went to all the strip shows with their myriad variations, grew to like pink, sweet horsemeat, and shared with the famous authors their *nostalgie de la boue*, a quality that Kawabata once phrased as "a taste for back streets." Was I an occupying imperialist indulging my vile colonial desires?

Probably. How many times, I wonder, did I take the Ginza line to the very end and surface into this sexy stratum, redolent of oysters over rice, camellia hair oil, cotton candy, underarm sweat. Dozens, each time led by the lure; rarely experiencing a real strike but always getting hooked.

The bait of Asakusa was the bribe of authenticity. My orderly Allied Occupation world seemed but a narrow veneer laid over this teeming land now so thriving with ambition and hope. There it was all rules and regulations. Here it was fortuitous, random, real. No one much smiled in my Army newspaper office, but in Asakusa there were lots of smiles—some of them cunning, others not. I would bask in this human warmth, and when I, probably by now myself smelling of pickled radish, took the subway back, it was with a sense of loss, as though I was leaving some state of happy innocence, some postwar Garden of Eden.

❋

I have not now for many years experienced that romantic notion, and the reason is that this Asakusa no longer exists. Progress did it in. Oh, Asakusa's still there on the map of

Tokyo, and the Ginza subway still ends there, but not that indulgent labyrinth, that pleasure warren that I used to pull over my head.

The Nakamise now sells tourist kitsch in the hope of turning a sale or two, the site of the Denkikan holds a Japanesque apartment block with an impoverished beauty-shop boutique on the ground floor. Buildings still stand awkwardly around vacant lots, but this is not because of destructive war but because of the peacetime price of land, the towering taxes, the ruinous loans.

The merry-go-round has disappeared, and just as vanished are the pleasure-seekers of old Asakusa. People now come only on holidays—at New Year's to Senso-ji, the temple reconstructed in painted ferroconcrete, on Sundays for the weekend racetrack betting compound.

Otherwise, silence, emptiness. In its determined march to the West, Tokyo's "heart" has simply left Asakusa behind, back in the East, down by the muddy river. Tokyoites still play, but they now do so in the boîtes of Omote-sando and the boutiques of Harajuku.

Asakusa makes sporadic efforts to recall some of this vanished attention. Gentrification, that last-ditch appeal, has been attempted. All the extant old temple pavilions have been segregated to a hopefully Disneyland-like location behind Senso-ji. Uprooted from their historical environment, they stand as though staring in consternation, and the several real Edo structures now appear just as phony as the plastic-looking replicas next to them.

There is now not only the Denkikan Mansion, an apartment-house complex, but also a plaque observing, among others, the dead comedian Enoken. A small street has been rusticated with Olde Nippon plastic cherry blossoms and fairy lanterns. Jinrikshas are being pulled about, providing jobs for local youths. And the Rokku (once six blocks of drama, sword fights, motion-picture palaces) now calls itself the Rox, hiding behind this trendy title all the empty lots, the torn-down theaters, the flashy façades ("Beaux Arts: We Sell a Tasty Life"), the fact that little life is left.

In these sixty years the level of national health has gone up, people have begun to live longer, have more money. Tokyo rose from the ashes, but Japan has paid a price for its progress. The sense of hope and possibility that Asakusa so embodied is now in short supply everywhere. If one desires an allegorical tableau of the downside of the Japanese "economic miracle," an opportunity is offered in Asakusa.

The district survived the 1923 earthquake, the reign of the Japanese military, World War II, the 1945 fire bombings—but it was finally killed off by the outbreak of peace, and is now reduced to its present corpse, the elegiac lament its only unguent.

❋

Such thoughts occupied me as I turned north and went to see what was left of the Yoshiwara, the nightless city, the famous pleasure city of old Edo. I was surprised to see the *mikaeri yanagi* still there, that famous willow tree at the gate. It was called that ("the reluctance-to-leave willow") because, passing under the great gate, you were supposed to regret having to leave the beauty, the pleasure, and all that wonderful flesh.

I had been surprised to find it still there the first time I went. That was early 1947, and the Yoshiwara, like the rest of Tokyo, had, after all, been bombed. That fabulous night city had gone up in smoke a year and a half before, and yet it was now open for business again—if on a more modest scale—and the willow was still there, though the great gate itself was gone.

There were new houses, mostly lathe and plaster, and a few older ones that had escaped the flames. The grid-straight streets of the quarter still had craters where great pleasure palaces had stood, but even here was the lemon sheen of new lumber and the scent of fresh-cut wood. Like everywhere else, the city was reemerging from its ashes.

And ready for commerce. The houses had young women looking out of the windows, and older women by the doors cajoling the passers-by. The place was brisk and businesslike, there was a sense of community, like that found everywhere in Japan in 1947.

And a belief in the future. Occupied though they were, the Japanese—delivered from war, they thought forever—saw new hope: do your utmost, put your best foot forward, democracy is just around the corner. Here, too, in the busy bustle of the Yoshiwara, optimism and expectation were palpable.

And as I strolled there, sixty years ago, I thought of what the place had once been, long before I initially saw it: a small civilization devoted to the pleasures of the flesh. Founded in Edo (now Tokyo) in 1617, it had flourished for almost three and a half centuries.

❋

Kyoto might have its Shimabara, Osaka its Shinmachi, but Tokyo's Yoshiwara was the most celebrated. Here, in an area of nearly twenty acres, lived an estimated 3,000 prostitutes—along with attendants, entertainers, masseurs, purveyors, servants, and various hangers-on. Yet, though called a *yukaku* (play quarter), it must have appeared more prison than playground. There were strong walls, moat-like creeks, gates, guards, curfews.

Though licensed prostitution was legal in Japan, there was, as always, a perceived need for control. This way—in their own city, as it were—the women and their customers were easier for the authorities to oversee and consequently control.

An unintended result of all this security, however, was that in the stratified social structure of Edo-period Japan this section of the city became, paradoxically, one of the few places where the citizen was relatively free of repression. In giving license to the prostitute, the authorities also involuntarily gave it to her customer. A degree of freedom was allowed you in the quarter that you did not enjoy in your own neighborhood.

Thus, while the Yoshiwara might certainly seem repressive to its inhabitants, visitors were freed, for a time, of social restraint. Rank no longer ruled. Merchants, farmers, artisans—even samurai if sufficiently disguised—could conspicuously mingle. Money was all that mattered.

And from this mingling came merchandising. Everything fashionable came from the quarter. Trends in clothing (a certain shade of beige, stripes in the summer), in manners, in parlance; styles in etiquette, in deportment, all came from the Yoshiwara. These were *iki* (cool), and woodblock print artists beautified the women and romanticized what happened in bed. The popular press turned on Yoshiwara wit, songs of the day dilated the talents of the denizens, the literature turned out picaresque accounts, including guide books to the best brothels, places where you could really get your money's worth.

And where you could spend inordinate amounts of it. Getting to the Yoshiwara, an hour's journey up the Sumida River by boat, or longer by palanquin or rickshaw, was just the beginning of the expense. Sex was never cheap in Japan.

Still, there you were, and the nightless city lay before you, a blaze of light, willows and cherry blossoms prettily contending, a pleasure-maze, a city within a city, a whole country with its own laws, its own customs, a nocturnal civilization. How grand it must have been—if one were a man.

Not for the women, however. Though some chose this life, others were sold into it by impoverished families. Like indentured servants, once in they found it difficult to get out. There had been a few improvements, though. The days when you could look at the girls through bars, as though in a zoo, when kidnappers and slave traders flourished, were long past. Modest reforms had been made. There was even a time, back in 1872, when prostitutes were declared legally free.

The general joy was soon extinguished, however, when they were declared still legally liable, still employees with contracts to fulfill. There was nothing to do but buy new licenses to continue their old trade, in order to pay off their mounting debts. The Yoshiwara was built to make money, and it made it both off the customers and the commodity.

When I first saw it in 1947, however, things were quite different. Much had been destroyed, and what remained seemed transmuted. Having lost a war, wiped clean the slate, Japan was ready for a better life. In a period of poverty, having a job, any job, was a virtue. The future was bright. Prostitution became, for a time, honest work. And with it came a sense of solidarity, as though the women were unionized. Their profession was legal.

The women I saw back then were engaged in a trade. It was one that perhaps they eventually wanted out of, but it offered something egalitarian, affirming, a belief in equal political, economic, social, and civil rights for everyone.

In its way this city of night had become a city of hope. Just as the Yoshiwara had earlier offered a zone free of the kind of social oppression so much a part of Edo life, it now offered a feeling of freedom, of optimism, in the midst of defeat and poverty.

When I passed the reluctance-to-leave willow on my way out, I thought that though the place might look seedy, it had about it a vitality, even a vivacity that matched that of the country itself. Here was a section of the city that could stand for the hope the old country seemed now to express.

So it was with curiosity that now I walked the half-hour from Asakusa, turned the corner, and found the willow — still there.

❖

It stood now not against a Kabuki-like avenue of grand houses with barred windows, as it had a hundred years ago; or a burned-out avenue of blackened ruins now filled with the yellow of new lumber, the smell of sawdust, the shouts of the workmen, the cries of the girls, as it had been sixty years ago; but, rather, I now saw it silhouetted against a backdrop of tallish modern buildings, many festooned with hanging lights or crowned by neon, most of them flashing names like *Yanagi* (willow), *Puriti Garu* (pretty girl), or simply and generically, *Sopurando* (soap-land).

The Yoshiwara, its activities quite illegal now, has transformed itself into an enormous bathing establishment — dozens of sauna-like enterprises where the ancient trade goes on under the guise of getting clean.

These were originally called, as elsewhere, Turkish baths—*toruko* had become the most common term of reference. But in 1984 a Turkish diplomat complained, and the Japanese government, wanting to renew its ban on prostitution, took the complaint seriously. So did those who ran the baths, and so a typical compromise was arranged.

The Tokyo-to Tokushu Yokujo Kyokai (Tokyo Special Bathhouses Association)—there is one—met and then announced that the more than one hundred affiliated bathhouses were amenable to a change of designation.

But to what? A democratic method was devised—the public, appealed to, responded with numerous suggestions. More than 2,000 postcards arrived. Among the contenders were Colt (that is Koruto, a backward rendering of toruko,) and Rabuyu (a felicitous combination of "love bath" and "love you") but the winner, hands down, was Sopurando, or Soapland.

The simplicity of its construction apparently appealed — a suggestion of cleanliness, soap; and a proposal of pleasure, Disneyland.

Instant was the success of the choice. The Turkish diplomat who had originally complained attended the inauguration of the new term and shook hands all around.

Prices then rose to match the level of dignity of the new title, and more efficient money-making methods were invented. Calling out your "attendant" by name now costs a bit more; there appears on the bill an unexplained but dignified *atobari* (unspecified charges when you check out); and the categories of attention are strictly insisted upon. There are special service, double service, extra special services, and full service — the last being what we call making love. There are also some expensive novelties. One example is the "fashion massage," a service that formerly the patron had practiced upon himself.

So it had come to this — this parody of a paradise. Yet, something has remained. Though the optimism and good will that I saw in 1947 is long evaporated, there is still the lasting smell of prostitution, strong a hundred years ago and reeking yet.

This is apparent as I watch. Taxis are greeted by men in suits with brush cuts and military bows. The few passers-by are cajoled by men with flashy ties. I look for missing little fingers but am too far away; however, I can recognize the general stance of the yakuza, the men who control crime here, the local mafia. They may have looked different a hundred years ago, but their equivalents were here. And so—then as now—the women who work for them.

These I cannot see. They are locked up inside the neon topped high-rises. And not all of them are there against their will. To some this is just a job, and a chosen one. But there are, as there were a century ago, those whose debts run high and whose escape is unlikely. The inmates have to buy their necessities from the proprietors—the soap, the towels. These are, quite frankly, criminally expensive. Their cost is put toward that grand total that must be paid if the worker is to be released.

I think of Chikamatsu, the famous Japanese playwright who specialized in stories of debt-burdened prostitutes in Edo's Yoshiwara or Osaka's Sakai and the tragedies (suicide usually) that met their efforts of escape. Living history lives on.

With some differences. Now many of the "girls" are not Japanese. They are Chinese or Korean (or more exotically, Baltic, Russian), who came to Japan to work and mostly did not know that they would end up in work like this.

I don't know about the Yoshiwara, but I do know that in Shinjuku, now Tokyo's major night city, their passports are taken away, and their return tickets, that they are burdened with mounting "debts," and that there they languish still.

And something else. Looking at the garish lights, all this advertisement, I see that the streets are empty. The festive Yoshiwara, with its evening crowds (even in 1947, let alone 1847), has vanished. Instead, a few taxis, some people climbing out or climbing in, the clustered yakuza underlings, the insouciant cop on the beat. The Yoshiwara is gone.

I think of the difference between then and now, I make some effort to equalize it. *Well, probably less women are unhappy now than then.* Thoughts like this. Or: *Well, at least they can get to the doctor more easily.* I search for reasons to make the present not only different but, in some way, better.

The impulse is recognizable. I do not want to believe in entropy, that measure of disorder that exists in a system—in this case the system called life. And beneath it I begin to detect another schism in myself. I am not certain about what I think of all this.

I may feel sorry for the sexually captive people, as I think I am sorry for the exploited paradisiacal native, but I detect the curve of the disingenuous, that slippery slope that gives a false impression of sincerity or simplicity.

What I want to feel and what I do feel are not identical. I turn again, as often, to Flaubert, and I find a passage: "It may be a perverted taste, but I love prostitution, and for itself, too, quite apart from its carnal aspects. . . . The idea of prostitution is a meeting place of so many elements—lust, bitterness, complete absence of human contact, muscular frenzy, the clink of gold—that to peer into it deeply makes one reel. One learns so many things in a brothel, and feels such sadness, and dreams so longingly of love. . . ."

❀

On my way out I pass again the *mikaeri yanagi*, the reluctance-to-leave willow, and recognize that my reluctance to leave is to be measured by my resistance to change. Yet, that is stupid—things change.

Is this to be regretted? No, but its results ought to be observed. Maybe that is what I am up to: memorializing change, celebrating transience by displaying what is left; traveling toward the future, eyes firmly on the past, living in the caboose.

And I again remember Cavafy:

> Keep Ithaka always in your mind.
> Arriving there is what you're destined for.
> But don't hurry the journey at all.
> Better that it lasts for years,
> so you're old by the time you reach the island. . . .

Feeling better, I continue down the darkened street, going home.